LIFESTYLE ARCHITECT

HOW TO: BUILD A LIFE OF PURPOSE, FREEDOM AND SUSTAINABLE HAPPINESS

BY SHU

Zen Remedy Lifestyle Architecture
Anchorage, Ak
1-888-818-1643
MyZenRemedy.com

PREFACE

How to Build a Life of Purpose, Freedom, and Sustainable Happiness' *isn't just a book; it's a transformative tool.*

A tool that can usher in positive global and generational change by first transforming the individual. The author recognizes there is no need to 'fix' the world externally; instead, if each one of us embarks on a journey to embrace and embody our authentic selves, the ripple effect will cultivate a world of unparalleled beauty and harmony.

Designed for self-discovery, its potency is amplified when incorporated into structured environments.

1. **Educational and Workplace Setting**: It's an invaluable asset for educators and facilitators in schools and workplaces, offering insights that foster deep personal growth. Engage with it in academic or professional environments, preferably under the guidance of a trained facilitator, to dive deep into its intricate lessons.

2. **Counseling & Coaching**: Therapists, counselors, and life coaches will find it a complementary tool for their practices, facilitating profound breakthroughs for clients.

3. **Lifestyle Architecture Program**: For those eager for a complete self-guided overhaul, look for the 'Lifestyle Architecture' online program – it pairs seamlessly with this book, enhancing your learning journey. Dive in and be the architect of your best life.

Through the pages of this book, you will discover how to cultivate a growth mindset, build healthy habits, design your environment, and create meaningful connections with others. You will also learn how to tap into your intuition, embrace uncertainty, and navigate challenges with grace and resilience.

In the chapters ahead, we will embark on a transformative journey of self-exploration and discovery. We will dive deep into the realms of introspection, drawing upon ancient wisdom, modern science, and practical exercises to help you uncover the unique tapestry of your purpose.

Together, we will weave a vibrant and inspiring lifestyle blueprint that reflects your truest self—a life designed with intention, authenticity, and the enduring commitment to your own happiness.

Are you ready to embark on this extraordinary quest of self-discovery and define your life purpose?

Prepare to unlock the doors of possibility, awaken your innermost dreams, and design a life that radiates purpose, freedom, and sustainable happiness.

1.
LIFESTYLE ARCHITECTURE

Elements to Consider in Lifestyle Architecture

In the vast landscape of life, we find ourselves continuously striving for a sense of purpose, freedom, and sustainable happiness. Just as an architect meticulously plans and constructs a building, we too can approach our lives with the mindset of a designer, creating a blueprint for a fulfilling existence. Welcome to the journey of Lifestyle Architecture.

To embark on this journey, we will draw inspiration from Jacques Fresco's five elements of architecture: overall functionality, efficiency or ease of assembly, aesthetics, sustainability, and adaptability. These principles, typically applied to the design of physical structures, provide a valuable framework for shaping our own lifestyles. By consciously integrating these elements into our lives, we can cultivate a harmonious balance that supports our goals and aspirations.

1. **Overall Functionality**:
The foundation of any well-designed lifestyle is its functionality. Just as an architect considers the purpose and function of each room in a building, we should reflect on the various aspects of our lives. What are the essential elements we desire in our daily routines, relationships, career, and personal growth? By understanding our unique needs, strengths, and values, we can create a framework that aligns with our deepest desires and aspirations.

2. Efficiency or Ease of Assembly:

Efficiency is key to optimizing our lifestyle design. We must seek simplicity and clarity in our choices, minimizing unnecessary complexities and distractions. By streamlining our routines, organizing our priorities, and eliminating non-essential commitments, we can create more time and space for what truly matters. Efficiency also extends to our decision-making process, encouraging us to make informed choices that propel us towards our goals and increase our overall well-being.

3. Aesthetics:

Just as a beautifully designed building uplifts our spirits, an aesthetically pleasing lifestyle can enhance our sense of joy and fulfillment. The aesthetics of our lives encompass both the physical and intangible elements. It involves cultivating an environment that inspires and nurtures us, from our living spaces to the art and objects that surround us. It also encompasses the beauty we create through our actions, relationships, and personal growth. By infusing beauty and artistry into every aspect of our lives, we can experience a profound sense of satisfaction and contentment.

Jacque Fresco 1916-2017
Was a futurist, designer, and social engineer who
co-founded The Venus Project

4. **Sustainability**:

Sustainability is not solely reserved for the realm of environmental conservation. It also applies to the way we design our lifestyles. A sustainable lifestyle emphasizes balance and harmony, acknowledging the interconnectedness of all things. It encompasses practices that nurture our physical, mental, and emotional well-being while considering the long-term impact on our planet and future generations. By embracing conscious consumption, mindful choices, and ethical decision-making, we can create a lifestyle that supports our well-being and preserves the world we inhabit.

5. **Adaptability:**

In the ever-changing tapestry of life, adaptability is crucial. Just as buildings must withstand the test of time, our lifestyles should possess the flexibility to evolve and respond to shifting circumstances. By cultivating adaptability, we develop resilience, enabling us to navigate challenges, embrace new opportunities, and grow as individuals. An adaptable lifestyle allows us to remain open to new experiences, perspectives, and paths, ultimately leading us towards a more fulfilling and purposeful existence.

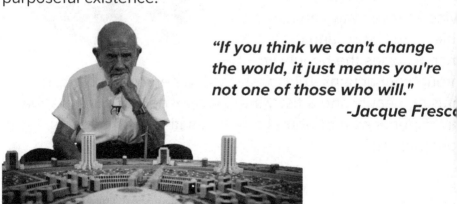

"If you think we can't change the world, it just means you're not one of those who will."
-Jacque Fresco

WITHIN THE CHAPTERS THAT FOLLOW, WE WILL GO DEEPER INTO EACH OF THESE ELEMENTS, EXPLORING HOW TO <u>BLUEPRINT</u> OUR IDEAL LIFESTYLE, <u>CONSTRUCT</u> IT WITH INTENTION, <u>APPRAISE</u> ITS CONGRUENCE WITH OUR VALUES, AND <u>MAINTAIN</u> ITS SUSTAINABILITY AND GROWTH.

Together, we will embark on an empowering journey, discovering the tools, strategies, and insights to design a life of purpose, freedom, and sustainable happiness.

2.

THE BLUEPRINT

Welcome to the world of lifestyle architecture, where you become the master of your own life design. In this chapter, we'll explore how to create a blueprint for someone's lifestyle that's grounded in purpose, freedom and sustainable happiness.

Just like an architect plans a building, you can plan your life with intention and attention to detail. With the right approach, you can create a lifestyle that aligns with your values, leverages your strengths, and propels you towards your goals.

Whether you're feeling stuck, unfulfilled, or simply seeking more meaning in your life, this chapter will guide you through the process of **crafting a blueprint** for a lifestyle that's uniquely suited to you. So, let's dive in and start building the life you truly desire!

1. **CREATE A VISION**
2. **ESTABLISH VALUES AND PRIORITIES**
3. **DEFINE A PURPOSE**
4. **CONDUCT A LIFESTYLE / BELIEFS AUDIT**
5. **DESIGN YOUR LIFESTYLE A *"SMARTER"* WAY**
6. **ECOLOGY**

"YOUR LIFE IS A BLANK CANVAS, AND YOU ARE THE ARTIST. IT IS UP TO YOU TO PAINT A BEAUTIFUL PICTURE BY CREATING A BLUEPRINT FOR THE LIFE YOU DESIRE." - AVIJEET DAS

CREATE A VISION

In the journey of self-discovery and designing a life of purpose, freedom, and sustainable happiness, the **first step in crafting a lifestyle blueprint is to create a vision**.

The power of a compelling vision cannot be overstated, as it acts as the guiding light that illuminates the path towards a fulfilling life. This chapter will examine the importance of creating a vision and its profound impact on our subconscious and reticular activating system, while highlighting the significance of allowing our hearts to lead the way during this transformative process.

Our subconscious mind is a remarkable reservoir of untapped potential, holding the key to unlocking our dreams and aspirations. It is like a vast ocean that stores our deepest desires, beliefs, and intentions, constantly influencing our thoughts, emotions, and actions. When we create a clear and vivid vision, we fine tune our subconscious mind directing its focus towards the realization of our deepest desires.

RETICULAR ACTIVATING SYSTEM (R.A.S.)

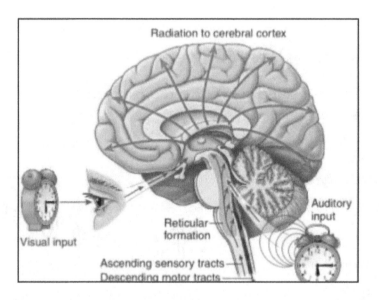

One remarkable aspect of our subconscious mind is the reticular activating system, a fascinating neurological mechanism that acts as a filter, selectively alerting us to information that aligns with our internal programming.

It's as if the universe conspires to support us on our journey, presenting us with synchronicities and serendipitous encounters that propel us towards our vision.

When we create a clear and compelling vision, we effectively reprogram our reticular alarm system to identify and amplify the elements of our surroundings that align with our aspirations and desires. By setting a vivid and intentional vision, we train our reticular activating system to attune itself to the opportunities, resources, and experiences that bring us closer to our desired lifestyle.

In essence, our reticular activating system acts as a personalized reality builder, shaping our perception of the world around us. It selectively draws our attention to the people, situations, and circumstances that resonate with our vision, making them more prominent in our conscious awareness. It is through this mechanism that the power of our vision becomes amplified, as we start noticing the signs, synchronicities, and opportunities that support our journey towards a life of purpose and fulfillment.

By understanding the role of the reticular activating system in constructing our version of reality, we gain an appreciation for the profound influence our vision holds.

Neuroplasticity Is our brains ability to adapt and alter thinking. It illuminates the elegant simplicity of the human brain's adaptability. To rewrite our subconscious programming, we don't need intricate interventions—merely shifting away from entrenched paths and patterns, and concentrating on fresh directions and perspectives.

Yet, this very simplicity is often the hardest thing for many to embrace. We, as humans, tend to overcomplicate matters, perhaps out of a belief that complexity signifies profundity. However, sometimes the most profound transformations arise from the simplest shifts in our thoughts and actions.

WHILE THE R.A.S. AND MIND ARE GREAT AT FILTERING OUR REALITY, WHEN IT COMES TO CREATING A VISION, IT IS CRUCIAL TO LET THE HEART DO THE TALKING.

While our logical mind and R.A.S. play important roles in decision-making and problem-solving, it is the heart that holds the deepest wisdom, intuition, and passion.

The heart knows what truly brings us joy, fulfillment, and purpose. By allowing ourselves to tap into our emotions, desires, and authentic yearnings, we create a vision that resonates with our deepest values and priorities.

As we engage in the process of creating a vision, it is essential to give ourselves permission to dream big, to envision a life that surpasses our current circumstances and limitations.

The vision acts as a bridge between our present reality and our future possibilities, our heart's desires with our physical condition. It empowers us to envision a life that aligns with our true potential and ignites our enthusiasm, fueling the motivation and perseverance necessary to overcome obstacle and setbacks along the way.

In "The Biology of Belief," Bruce Lipton illustrates the vast difference between our conscious and subconscious processing abilities, with *the subconscious managing around 40 million bits of information compared to the mere 40 bits our conscious mind handles*.

This dichotomy introduces the concept of the reticular alarm system, a mental filter that shapes our reality by focusing on what we deem essential. If this system is not attuned to recognize specific opportunities or truths, they may remain invisible to us, creating a "scotoma" or a mental blind spot.

This phenomenon underscores the importance of mindful self-awareness and intention in shaping our life's direction. It's a reminder that programming our consciousness towards purpose, freedom, and sustainable happiness might reveal pathways previously hidden to us.

We will now explore practical techniques and exercises to help you craft a compelling and inspiring vision for your lifestyle blueprint.

Afterwards, we will delve into the process of establishing values and priorities, defining your purpose, conducting a lifestyle and beliefs audit, designing your lifestyle in a "SMARTER" way, and finish up with and ecology check to make sure all parts fit good together.

By following these steps, you will be ready to lay the foundation for a life that is deeply meaningful, purpose-driven, and aligned with your authentic self.

TOOLS FOR CREATING YOUR VISION

To help you develop and articulate your vision, check out these tools and methods to aid in the process of self-reflection and goal setting.

Vision board: A vision board is a collage of images, words, and phrases that represent your goals and dreams. It's a visual representation of what you want to achieve in your life, and can help you stay focused and motivated.

Mind mapping: Mind mapping is a technique that involves creating a diagram to visually organize your thoughts and ideas. It can be a useful tool for brainstorming, planning, and setting goals.

Journaling: Writing down your thoughts and feelings can be a powerful tool for self-reflection and goal setting. You can use a journal to track your progress, identify areas for improvement, and celebrate your successes.

It can also allow our emotions to be released in a way that is like unplugging a pipe. When we allow ourselves to feel negative emotions with journaling, our positive emotions can flow more freely.

Journaling acts as a cathartic outlet, providing a safe space to express and process challenging emotions. By acknowledging and confronting our negative feelings, we create room for positivity to thrive.

Moreover, journaling offers a unique opportunity for self-discovery and self-awareness. As we journey into our thoughts and experiences on paper, we gain insights into our own patterns, beliefs, and values. This newfound understanding enables us to make informed decisions, set meaningful goals, and cultivate a sense of purpose.

Journaling fosters a balanced emotional landscape, allowing us to embrace both the ups and downs of life with greater resilience and gratitude.

Meditation: Meditation can help you quiet your mind, focus your thoughts, and visualize your goals. It's a powerful tool for reducing stress and anxiety, improving concentration, and increasing self-awareness.

Meditation can be understood in the context of the yin/ yang, two opposite poles.

In: The first pole involves concentrated focus, where practitioners direct their attention to a specific idea, color, mantra, or object. This focused meditation cultivates a deep sense of concentration and helps quiet the mind by anchoring it to a single point of focus.

By immersing oneself in this concentrated state, individuals can explore the depths of their chosen subject, enhancing their understanding and connection to it.

Out: On the other pole is the practice of complete quieting or letting go. This form of meditation involves releasing the incessant chatter of the mind, often referred to as the "chattering monkey." Through this practice, individuals aim to enter a state of pure awareness and presence, where the mind becomes still and thoughts arise and pass without attachment.

This meditative state allows for a deep sense of relaxation, inner peace, and a heightened connection to the present moment.

A simple protocol for belly breathing to coastal breathing can be practiced as follows:

1. ***Find a comfortable and quiet place*** to sit or lie down. Close your eyes and bring your attention to your breath.

2. ***Begin by focusing on your abdominal breathing.*** Place your hands on your abdomen and feel it rise and fall with each breath. Inhale deeply through your nose, allowing your abdomen to expand fully. Exhale slowly through your mouth, feeling your abdomen contract. Repeat this belly breathing for a few minutes, allowing your breath to become slow and deep.

3. ***After establishing a steady rhythm of abdominal breathing, shift your focus to coastal breathing.*** Now, direct your attention to the rise and fall of your chest as you breathe. Inhale deeply through your nose, feeling your chest expand outward. Exhale slowly through your mouth, allowing your chest to relax and fall. Continue this coastal breathing for a few minutes, maintaining a smooth and relaxed breath.

4. ***Finally, if you wish to deepen your practice***, you can transition to full yogic breathing. Inhale deeply through your nose, expanding your abdomen first, then your chest, and finally filling your upper lungs. Exhale slowly, releasing the breath in reverse order: first from the upper lungs, then the chest, and finally contracting your abdomen. Repeat this full yogic breath for a few cycles, allowing yourself to fully experience the rhythmic flow of your breath.

Remember, as you practice this protocol, try to maintain a relaxed and gentle state of mind. If your attention wanders, gently bring it back to your breath. Gradually, with consistent practice, you can cultivate a sense of inner calm and balance through the power of breathing.

Ultimately, the most important thing is to find the tool or combination of tools that work best for you. Experiment with different techniques and see what helps you visualize your life goals most effectively.

ESTABLISH VALUES AND PRIORITIES

At the core of our blueprint lies a deep understanding of our values and priorities—the guiding principles that shape our choices, actions, and ultimately, our overall satisfaction in life.

In this section, we embark on a transformative exercise that delves into our subconscious, unveiling hidden sources of contentment and fulfillment. By engaging in this exercise, we will gain valuable insights that wi enable us to prioritize our aspirations and forge a meaningful path forward.

Additionally, we will introduce you to an array of powerful tools and techniques that will help you know and articulate your values, empowering you to create a lifestyle blueprint tha reflects your authentic desires and leads you towards a life of profound fulfillment.

WHAT ARE YOU PASSIONATE ABOUT?

WHEEL OF LIFE EXERCISE

In the journey of self-discovery and designing a life of purpose, freedom, and sustainable happiness, it is crucial to understand our values and priorities.

What truly matters to us?

What areas of our life are we most satisfied with

Which ones are in need of attention and growth?

To help answer these questions, we introduce you to an insightful exercise called the Wheel of Life.

The Wheel of Life exercise serves as a mirror reflecting the current state of our existence. It allows us to gauge how fulfilled we are in various aspects, including family, finances, business, education, spirituality, health, fun, community, travel, and social connections.

By working through this exercise, you will gain valuable insights into where you stand in each area and identify potential areas for refinement and enhancement.

Exercise guidelines:

▶ **Work quickly:** The purpose of this exercise is to tap into your subconscious mind, allowing it to speak over your conscious thinking mind. To achieve this, it is essential to work swiftly. The longer you take, the more your conscious thoughts may influence your responses, potentially creating a false read.

▶ **Draw dots:** As you evaluate each aspect, draw a dot on the line connecting the number 1 in the middle to 10 near the arrow. The position of the dot represents your level of satisfaction with that particular aspect. Place the dot closer to 1 if you are less satisfied and closer to 10 if you are more satisfied.

▶ **Connect the dots:** Once you have drawn all ten dots, connect them with a line. The resulting shape will provide a visual representation of your satisfaction levels across different areas of life. The rounder the shape, the smoother your ride in life may be, indicating a relatively balanced and harmonious existence.

Keep in mind that using a fresh page for each session prevents any bias or preconceptions from influencing your evaluation. This way, your mind remains open and receptive to the true reflection of your current state.

The Wheel of Life exercise is a powerful tool for self-reflection, self-discovery, and self-directed growth. It provides valuable insights into the areas of your life that may need attention, guiding you toward a more purposeful and balanced existence.

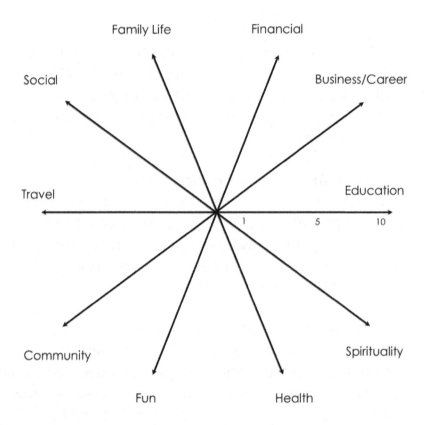

Take the opportunity to explore this exercise and let it be a compass on your journey towards designing a life of purpose, freedom, and sustainable happiness.

<u>The Wheel of Life exercise offers several benefits:</u>

1. ***Identifying priorities:*** By assessing your satisfaction levels in each area, you can discern which aspects of life hold greater significance for you. This exercise acts as a guide, indicating where you might want to focus your energy and attention to create a more satisfying and fulfilling life.

2. ***Establishing a starting point:*** The completed Wheel of Life provides a snapshot of your current situation. It offers a clear visual representation of where you stand and helps you gauge your starting point for personal growth and transformation.

3. ***Accessing the subconscious:*** The Wheel of Life exercise enables you to tap into your subconscious mind. Requiring swift responses, it bypasses conscious overthinking and allows deeper insights to emerge. You can use this exercise repeatedly to access your subconscious and gain further clarity.

4. ***Tracking personal growth:*** Some individuals find enjoyment in using the same page over and over, observing how their Wheel of Life shifts over time. Each iteration becomes a testament to their personal growth and serves as a reminder of the progress made.

Now Please take a moment to reflect on and provide your beliefs and thoughts on the following facets of life. There is no need to use a rating scale; simply express your opinions and perspectives on each topic. Your responses will help us gain a better understanding of your views and values.

Family:

▶ How would you describe the importance of family in your life?

_____

▶ What role do family members play in your decision-making process?

_____

▶ How do you define a healthy family dynamic?

_____

▶ How do you prioritize spending time with your family?

_____

Education:

▶ What value do you place on education and learning?

_____

▶ What are your goals and aspirations when it comes to education?

_____

▶ How do you believe education contributes to personal growth and development?

_____

▶ How would you define a successful educational journey?

_____

Financial:

▶ How do you perceive the role of money in your life?

_____

▶ What are your financial goals and objectives?

_____

▶ How do you approach financial planning and budgeting?

_____

▶ What does financial security mean to you?

_____

Social:

▶ How do you define the importance of social connections and relationships?

_____

▶ How do you maintain and foster meaningful social connections?

_____

▶ What role do you believe social activities and gatherings play in your life?

_____

▶ How do you balance your social life with other aspects of your life?

_____

Career:

▶ How do you view the significance of a career in your life?

_____

▶ What factors are important to you in choosing a career path?

_____

▶ How do you define success in your professional life?

_____

▶ How do you strike a balance between work and personal life?

_____

Travel:

▶ What does travel mean to you?

_____

▶ How do you prioritize travel in your life?

_____

▶ What are your favorite travel experiences or destinations?

_____

▶ How do you believe travel contributes to personal growth and understanding?

_____

Spirituality:

▶ How would you describe your spiritual beliefs or worldview?

_____

▶ How do you practice or engage with your spirituality?

_____

▶ How do you see spirituality influencing other areas of your life?

_____

▶ How do you find meaning and purpose in life?

_____

Community:

▶ How important is community involvement to you?

_____

▶ How do you contribute to your community?

_____

▶ What benefits do you see in being an active member of a community?

_____

▶ How do you believe community support impacts individual well-being?

_____

Fun:

▶ What activities or hobbies bring you joy and fulfillment?

_____

▶ How do you incorporate fun and leisure into your daily life?

_____

▶ How do you define a balanced and enjoyable lifestyle?

_____

▶ What role does fun play in your overall well-being?

_____

Health:

▶ How do you prioritize your physical and mental health?

_____

▶ What habits or practices do you engage in to maintain your health?

_____

▶ How do you view the connection between physical and mental well-being?

_____

▶ What does a healthy lifestyle mean to you?

_____

In addition to the Wheel of Life exercise, there are various other methods and tools available online that can assist in revealing our values and priorities.

These resources offer different approaches to self-reflectio and personal growth, allowing individuals to delve deeper into their inner selves. Some options include self-reflection exercises, values clarification activities, values assessment surveys, seeking feedback from others, and engaging in professional coaching.

These tools, although some may require a fee and provide comprehensive guidance, offer valuable insights and support for those seeking to gain a clearer understanding of their core values and priorities, ultimately assisting in the process of designing a life aligned with their authentic selves.

Self-reflection: One of the most basic methods is to take time for self-reflection and introspection. This involves examining your thoughts, feelings, and actions to identify what values are most important to you. You can ask yourself questions like: *What motivates me? What makes me feel fulfilled? What do I stand for?*

Values clarification exercises: These are structured activities that help individuals identify their core values. There are different types of values clarification exercises, such as ranking values in order of importance, identifying values that resonate with you, or imagining your ideal self.

Values assessment surveys: There are several online surveys that can help you assess your values, such as the **Personal Values Assessment,** the **Values in Action Inventory,** and the **Schwartz Values Survey**. These surveys ask you to rate different values based on how important they are to you.

Feedback from others: Sometimes, it can be helpful to get feedback from others who know you well. They may be able to provide insights into your values based on their observations of your behavior and attitudes.

Professional counseling or coaching: A trained counselor or coach can help you identify and clarify your values. They can provide guidance and support as you navigate this process and help you align your values with your actions and goals.

OVERALL, IT IS IMPORTANT TO REMEMBER THAT EVALUATING OUR VALUES IS AN ONGOING PROCESS. AS WE GROW AND CHANGE, OUR VALUES MAY SHIFT, AND IT IS IMPORTANT TO REGULARLY ASSESS AND RE-EVALUATE WHAT IS MOST IMPORTANT TO US

DEFINE A PURPOSE

At the core of every individual lies a burning desire to lead a life of purpose, to find meaning in their existence, and to experience a sense of fulfillment. Defining a life purpose is the key that unlocks the door to a truly extraordinary existence. It is the compass that guides us through the labyrinth of choices and opportunities, illuminating our path toward a life of significance and sustainable happiness.

In this section, we investigate the profound importance of discovering and defining your life purpose. We will craft a beautiful personal life affirmation, a powerful statement that captures the essence of your purpose.

This affirmation will serve as a constant reminder of your truest desires, providing clarity and focus as you navigate the choices and challenges that life presents. It is a living document, one that can be refined and adapted as you grow and evolve on your journey.

Defining your purpose goes beyond mere words or intentions; it holds the potential to support the manifestation of your dreams and desires.

The act of defining your purpose will activate and support your reticular activating system, a powerful mechanism within your brain that filters and brings into focus the experiences and opportunities that align with your purpose.

By consciously clarifying and defining your purpose, you prime your reticular activating system to recognize and celebrate a congruent reality. As a result, you begin to notice synchronicities, serendipities, and opportunities that propel you toward a life of purpose and freedom.

ASK YOURSELF WHAT YOU CHOOSE TO ACHIEVE BY DESIGNING YOUR LIFESTYLE.

Do you choose to improve your health, career, relationships, or overall well-being? If nothing else your purpose could be a happy, stress-free life, for example.

Now with your heart and mind primed, meditate on the following guiding questions and write out your answers.

Perfection is not necessary, you can always fine tune later.

▶ What are my gifts and talents?
When you "dance" like when no one is watching".

_____

▶ What do I choose to create?
Answer this as though you its something you can "work like you don't need the money".

_____

▶ What am I passionate about?
What you love most with your heart, as if it has never been challenged.

_____

▶ What do I need to learn in order to have more love and joy in my life?
This may include skills, attributes, attitudes, disciplines and/or knowledge.

_____

▶ What empowers me?

_____

With the information gathered, complete the following
statement:

MY PURPOSE

I, _____ am here to apply
my gifts of

_____

in order to create

_____

With the passion of

_____

I learn

_____

and I am empowered with

_____

CONDUCT A LIFESTYLE/PROGRAMMING AUDIT

Just as an architect meticulously plans and designs a structure, we too have the power to shape and mold ou lives according to our own blueprint.

One fundamental step in this process is conducting a comprehensive lifestyle and programming audit. This audit serves as a vital tool to assess the current state of various factors that influence our lives, including medical, psychosocia and environmental aspects. By thoroughly examining these areas, we gain valuable insights into the areas that require attention, improvement, or transformation.

During this audit, we will not only scrutinize the external aspects of our lives but also delve into the intricate workings c our internal world. Our programs or beliefs, whether conscious or unconscious, play a significant role in shaping our thoughts, actions, and overall outlook on life. They form the foundation upon which we build our reality and make decisions that impact our well-being.

The protocol we will explore in this section is designed to guide us through the process of evaluating our beliefs and determining their value or worth in our lives. It is a structured approach to assess whether our current beliefs align with our goals, values, and aspirations.

By doing so, we can discern whether certain beliefs serve us well and contribute positively to our journey, or if they hinder our progress and hold us back from reaching our true potential.

Much like a software upgrade, we will assess our beliefs like they are programs, with the intention of deciding whether to keep, delete, or upgrade them. This process allows us to shed limiting programming that no longer serve us and embrace empowering ones that align with our authentic selves. It is a transformative process that enables us to consciously shape our mindset, actions, and the way we navigate through life.

As we embark on this journey of self-discovery and introspection, it is essential to **approach it with openness, curiosity, and a willingness to challenge our preconceived notions.**

By conducting a lifestyle and beliefs audit, we are designing a life that acknowledges our starting point.

Remember, the power to design your life lies within you. By undertaking this audit, you are taking a significant step towards crafting a life of purpose, freedom, and sustainable happiness.

Let us begin this transformative journey together, exploring the depths of our current lifestyle and beliefs, paving the way for a more fulfilling existence.

LIFESTYLE AUDIT

Medical History:

▶ Do you have any chronic health conditions (e.g. diabetes, high blood pressure, heart disease)?

_____

▶ Have you had any surgeries or hospitalizations in the past year?

_____

▶ Are you currently taking any medications or supplements?

_____

_____

_____

Lifestyle Habits:

▶ How many servings of fruits and vegetables do you eat each day?

_____

▶ How often do you eat fast food or processed snacks?

_____

▶ Do you have any dietary restrictions (e.g. gluten-free, vegetarian, vegan)?

_____

▶ How often do you enjoy playful activity or "exercise" each week?

_____

▶ How many hours of sleep do you get each night?

_____

▶ Do you smoke cigarettes or use other tobacco products?

_____

▶ How much alcohol do you consume in a typical week?

_____

Environmental Factors:

▶ Are you exposed to any toxins or pollutants in your work or living environment?

_____

▶ Do you have access to clean air and water where you live?

_____

▶ How often do you spend time in nature or green spaces?

_____

<u>Psychosocial Factors:</u>

▶ How would you rate your current level of stress on a scale of 1-10?

_____

▶ Do you have any mental health concerns (e.g. anxiety, depression, bipolar disorder)?

_____

▶ How often do you spend time with friends and family?

_____

▶ Do you have a support network that you can rely on?
_____

▶ What are your health and wellness goals?

_____

_____

_____

▶ What inspires you to make healthy lifestyle changes?

_____

▶ What obstacles have prevented you from achieving your goals in the past?

_____

_____

▶ Additional Comments
_Is there anything else you would like to share about your lifestyle
r health habits?_

_____

_____

CHAKRAS OR "BIOLOGICAL HARD-DRIVES"

In the realm of holistic well-being and personal growth, the concept of chakras holds significance.

Derived from ancient Indian traditions, chakras are believed to be energy centers within our subtle energetic body, corresponding to various aspects of our physical, emotional, and spiritual well-being.

Though their existence may be debated, reflecting on the concepts of chakras can still provide valuable insights for self-discovery.

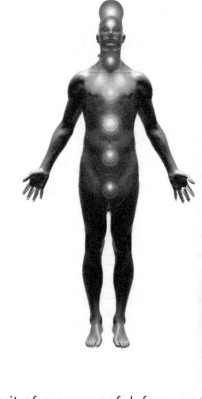

It is suggested that the state of our chakras can influence our physiology and overall sense of balance. Learning about the chakra system can reveal how the location of illness or distress may be related to specific areas of our life.

Understanding this metaphorical framework allows individuals to identify potential areas of fragmentation or illness, helping them prioritize and address these aspects in their pursuit of a purposeful, free, and sustainably happy life.

By considering chakras, even as symbolic representations, *one can metaphorically sweep away the cobwebs in their personal architecture,* fostering a greater sense of clarity and congruence within themselves.

By examining the chakra system and our physical symptoms, we can identify areas of our life that need attention and make necessary adjustments to bring ourselves back into alignment and congruence with our lifestyle blueprint.

Root Chakra:

Energetic imbalances in the root chakra, associated with stability and grounding, might manifest as problems related to the lower body, such as lower back pain, constipation, or immune system disorders.

▶ Do you feel grounded and connected to the earth?

_____

▶ Do you have a sense of stability and security in your life?

_____

▶ Do you feel safe and supported by your community?

_____

▶ Is there any group that you feel superior/inferior to or oppressed by?

_____

Sacral Chakra:

Disruptions in the sacral chakra, linked to creativity and emotional well-being, could potentially contribute to issues like reproductive system disorders, sexual dysfunctions, or hormonal imbalances.

▶ Do you feel creative and inspired in your daily life?

_____

▶ Do you have healthy relationships with yourself and others?

_____

▶ Do you feel comfortable expressing your emotions and desires?

_____

▶ What unproductive or destructive habits would you change about yourself?

_____

▶ Are your emotions well-balanced or do they swing from one extreme to another?

_____

▶ Are you satisfied with your sex life?

_____

Solar Plexus Chakra:

Imbalances in the solar plexus chakra, related to personal power and self-esteem, may be associated with digestive problems, ulcers, or disorders of the liver and pancreas.

▶ Do you have a strong sense of self-esteem and self-worth?

_____

▶ Are you able to set healthy boundaries with others?

_____

▶ Do you feel confident and empowered in your life?

_____

▶ Are you able to be assertive when necessary?

_____

▶ What are your favorite characteristics about yourself?

_____

▶ What traits would you change about yourself?

_____

▶ Your major accomplishments are?

_____

▶ What issue or challenge has a pattern of blocking or slowing your successes?

_____

<u>Heart Chakra:</u>

Energetic disharmony in the heart chakra, representing love and compassion, might potentially affect the cardiovascular system, manifesting as heart conditions, high blood pressure, or respiratory issues.

▶ Do you feel connected to your heart and your innermost desires?

_____

▶ Do you have loving and supportive relationships with others?

_____

▶ Are you able to forgive yourself and others for past hurts?

_____

▶ Have you wronged somebody?

_____

▶ Has someone wronged you?

_____

▶ Is there anyone you resent?

_____

▶ What are you passionate about?

_____

▶ Is your passion expressed in a healthy way?

_____

Throat Chakra:

Imbalances in the throat chakra, associated with communication and self-expression, may potentially contribute to throat infections, thyroid disorders, or problems with the neck and shoulders.

▶ Do you feel able to express yourself clearly and authentically?

_____

▶ Do you listen to and honor your own needs and desires?

_____

▶ Do you feel confident in your ability to communicate with others?

_____

▶ Are there others that you can trust without doubt?

_____

▶ Do you gossip?

_____

▶ Are you holding something in that you need to confess?

_____

Third Eye Chakra:

Disruptions in the third eye chakra, linked to intuition and inner wisdom, could potentially influence neurological and sensory disorders, migraines, or issues with concentration and perception.

▶ Do you feel connected to your intuition and inner wisdom?

_____

▶ Are you able to see beyond surface-level appearances and understand deeper truths?

_____

▶ Do you feel aligned with your life purpose and spiritual path?

_____

▶ Are you well organized and have good planning skills?

_____

__Crown Chakra:__

Energetic imbalances in the crown chakra, representing spiritual connection and enlightenment, may be associated with psychological disorders, migraines, or general imbalances in the body's energy system.

▶ Do you feel connected to a higher power or universal energy?

_____

▶ Do you have a sense of transcendence and connection to the larger world around you?

_____

▶ Do you feel a sense of spiritual fulfillment and purpose in your life?

_____

▶ Do you put conditions towards your spiritual experience?

_____

▶ Do you reject divine guidance in its divine form?

_____

It is important to note that these examples are based on the holistic perspective of chakras, and their connection to physical health is subjective and not scientifically substantiated.

Nevertheless, contemplating these associations within the context of personal well-being can encourage self-reflection and exploration, leading individuals to prioritize and address various aspects of their lives.

This questionnaire is intended to be used as a starting point for a holistic lifestyle assessment that takes into account physical, emotional, and spiritual well-being.

Chakras can be likened to biological hard drives, storing and regulating the energetic information of our beings. Just as a computer's hard drive can become fragmented over time, leading to slower performance and system glitches, our chakras can also become imbalanced or misaligned due to emotional traumas, negative experiences, or physical illnesses. *This fragmentation manifests as disease or discomfort in our physical bodies*.

Defragmentation, in computer terms, involves reorganizing and realigning the stored information for optimal performance. Similarly, healing practices, such as *meditation, cognitive behavioral therapy, neurolinguistics programming, and holistic therapies*, serve as defragmentation processes for our chakras, restoring them to their optimal state and subsequently promoting health and balance in our physical form.

Just as the lifestyle audit allowed us to assess and evaluate our external circumstances, the beliefs or programming audit invites us to introspect and examine the internal landscapes of our minds and hearts.

Our program, whether conscious or subconscious, shapes our perception, influences our choices, and ultimately determines the direction of our lives.

PROGRAMMING AUDIT

In this section, we will continue on a profound journey of self-reflection, unraveling the threads of our deeply ingrained beliefs, questioning their origins, and discerning whether they truly serve our highest potential.

We are all constantly "downloading" new "programs". Bits of information are constantly becoming integrated into our whole being through the lives we experience and then into our beliefs.

Our **cultures, countries, parents, races, TV commercials, news, education, and streets** offer all forms of programming. Some programming keeps us safe, makes us smarter and wiser. Other programs can cripple our systems and even make them crash. Some things we are taught **can act as malware, spyware and viruses.**

With so much information available to us in our modern
ness how do we filter what will add to our development and
what will take away?

Our own subjectivity can sometimes keep us trapped in
oxic relationships and work environments. When we are driven
olely by our subjective perspectives, we may fail to recognize
he negative impact they have on our well-being.

The following is a tool to assess your group of beliefs or
our "programming". When a computer runs slow or crashes
ve scan the system for damaging software we also need to
can our own beliefs on a continuum in order to ensure the
ptimum operation of your Human Operating System.

▶ **Read the 3 principles of "Human
Programming"**

▶ **Examine and reflect on everything thing you
believe about life through the lens of the 5
criteria for beneficial "programs' or beliefs.**

▶ **If your "program" can hold up to at least
three or more criteria it is considered beneficial
to your Growth and Health.**

*If your program is not congruent with at least 3 of the 5
riteria, its time to get an "upgrade" or delete the program
ll together.*

3 PRINCIPLES "HUMAN PROGRAMMING" OR CONDITIONING

Having an objective criteria to evaluate our personal belief. or programming is valuable because it helps us assess whether they are beneficial or destructive towards our lifestyle blueprint.

The following are the three principles through which we are programmed:

1. **Beliefs:** Our conscious and unconscious acceptance of information as "true" forms the basis of our programming. These beliefs shape our behavior and moral values.

2. **Conditioning:** Our behavior and morals are influenced by what we consider to be true. Our conditioning plays a significant role in how we navigate through life.

3. **Individual Choice:** Each individual has the freedom to choose what they accept as true. *We have the power to select the beliefs that align with our values and aspirations.*

5 CRITERIA TO ASSESS THE VALUE OF A PROGRAM / BELIEF

To assess our own programming objectively, we can consider the following five-point evaluation:

1. **Alignment with Calling:** Does our belief or programming push us towards fulfilling our calling or divine programming (Dharma)? Is it Congruent with your *SMARTER* objectives discussed in next section.

2. **Life Protection:** Does it protect our life, ensuring our safety and well-being?

3. **Fact-Based:** Is it based on verifiable facts, supported by evidence and rationality?

4. **Avoidance of Fragmentation or Stress:** Does it prevent or resolve undesirable stress and fragmentation in our bodies and Chakras, which can be seen as our biological hard drives?

5. **Positive Feelings:** Does it attract feelings of peace and harmony, promoting overall well-being?

Take any belief you have about anything and run it through this protocol.

Remember, If your belief or program meet 3 or more of these criteria, they can be considered beneficial.

However, if they fall short, it may be necessary to upgrade to new beliefs that align better with the blueprint of our lives or even discard them altogether.

HEROS

Examining our heroes can offer valuable insights when it comes to establishing our beliefs, values, and priorities. Heroes serve as role models who inspire us with their exceptional qualities, actions, and achievements.

By closely analyzing our heroes, we can gain a deeper understanding of the qualities we admire, the principles we hold dear, and the goals we aspire to achieve. Reflecting on what makes them our heroes enables us to uncover the values and priorities that resonate with us on a personal level, providing guidance in shaping our own character and aspirations.

Your hero can be real or mythic, dead or alive. It's about the characteristics they display.

To reflect on what makes someone our hero, here are a few questions to consider:

Your Hero _____

1. What specific qualities or traits does my hero possess that I find admirable and inspiring?

_____

2. How have my hero's actions or achievements positively impacted others or made a difference in the world?

_____

3. In what ways does my hero embody the values and principles that I hold dear?

_____

4. How does my hero's journey or story resonate with my own experiences or aspirations?

_____

5. What lessons can I learn from my hero's successes, failures, or challenges?

_____

6. How does my hero's behavior align with my own moral compass and ethical beliefs?

_____

7. Do I share similar goals or ambitions with my hero, and if so, how can I work towards them?

_____

8. How does my hero inspire me to be a better version of myself or make a positive impact in my own life and the lives of others?

_____

9. Are there any aspects of my hero's character or actions that I disagree with or find problematic, and how does this shape my perspective on heroism and personal values?

_____

> By contemplating these questions and examining the heroes we admire, we can gain valuable insights into our own beliefs, values, and priorities, ultimately guiding us towards personal growth and a more fulfilling life.

DESIGN YOUR LIFESTYLE *SMARTER*

n our quest to design a life of purpose, freedom, and sustainable happiness, it is essential to set goals that are not only inspiring but also practical and achievable.

Now that you have **created a vision, defined your purpose, and established your values and priorities**, it's time to outline our objectives using the **SMARTER** method.

This section will guide you through the process of setting goals that are *Specific, Measurable, Achievable, Relevant, Time-lined, Enthusiastic, and Rewarding. (SMARTER)*

By incorporating these principles into your goal-setting practice, you will greatly enhance your chances of success and create a solid foundation for your lifestyle architecture.

SPECIFIC -

Clarity is Key

Setting specific goals is crucial for effective planning and execution. By clearly defining what you want to achieve, you can focus your energy and efforts more efficiently. Ask yourself the following questions:

▶ *What exactly do I want to accomplish?*

▶ *Why is this goal important to me?*

▶ *How will I know when I have achieved it?*

MEASURABLE -

Tracking Progress and Success

Measuring your progress allows you to stay motivated and make necessary adjustments along the way. When setting measurable goals, consider the following:

- ▶ *How will I measure my progress?*
- ▶ *What are the key milestones or indicators of success?*
- ▶ *Can I quantify my goal in terms of time, quantity, or another relevant metric?*

ACHIEVABLE -

Balancing Ambition and Reality

While it's important to dream big, it's equally vital to set goals that are within your reach. An achievable goal provides a sense of confidence and prevents discouragement. Consider the following when setting achievable goals:

- ▶ *Do I have the necessary resources and abilities to accomplish this goal?*
- ▶ *What steps can I take to acquire any missing resources or skills?*
- ▶ *Can I break down the goal into smaller, more manageable tasks?*

RELEVANT -

Aligning with Your Values and Aspirations

Relevance ensures that your goals are aligned with your overall vision and values. A relevant goal should resonate with your passions, interests, and long-term aspirations. Reflect on the following when setting relevant goals:

▶ *Does this goal align with my core values and beliefs?*

▶ *How does achieving this goal contribute to my overall vision of a purposeful, free, and happy life?*

▶ *Will this goal have a positive impact on my well-being and the well-being of others?*

TIME-LINED -

Setting Deadlines for Accountability

Adding a timeline to your goals brings a sense of urgency and accountability. Without a deadline, goals can easily be delayed or forgotten. When establishing timelines, consider the following:

▶ *When do I choose to achieve this goal?*

▶ *Are there any natural time constraints or external factors to consider?*

▶ *Can I break down the goal into smaller time-bound objectives?*

ENTHUSIASTIC -

Cultivating Passion and Motivation

Enthusiasm fuels your journey and keeps you inspired throughout the goal-setting process. Cultivating passion and excitement for your goals is vital for maintaining momentum. Consider the following:

> ▶ *How can I infuse enthusiasm into my goal-setting process?*
> ▶ *What aspects of this goal genuinely excite and energize me?*
> ▶ *How can I stay motivated when faced with challenges or setbacks?*

REWARDING -

Celebrating Milestones and Achievements

Rewarding yourself along the way is essential for maintaining a positive mindset and acknowledging your progress. By celebrating milestones and achievements, you reinforce positive habits and create a cycle of success. Reflect on the following:

> ▶ *How can I reward myself for achieving milestones or making progress?*
> ▶ *What forms of celebration align with my values and preferences?*
> ▶ *How can I maintain a sense of gratitude and acknowledge my achievements*

ECOLOGY

In the context of Neuro-Linguistic Programming (NLP), ecology refers to the study of the effects of any change in a system. It's about the balance and harmony of the system as a whole, and understanding that any change can potentially impact other areas of the system, whether it's a person's life, a company, or a community.

For example, a shift in a company's objective from employee satisfaction to solely profit maximization might initially lead to an increase in profits. However, this could also result in decreased employee morale, higher turnover, lower quality of work, and eventual harm to the company's reputation and profitability.

Similarly, in personal life, an individual might focus heavily on career advancement, neglecting their health or personal relationships in the process. While this might lead to short-term success, it could also result in long-term health problems or a lack of social support, which could negatively affect their overall happiness and quality of life.

Thus, understanding the concept of ecology is vital in making balanced, sustainable changes in any system. It highlights the interconnectedness of various aspects of life and the importance of considering the whole system when making decisions or implementing changes.

You're doing great 💪😁👍, it may seem like a lot of things to think about right now. *As you put this into practice, you'll find that it becomes more automatic <u>with every objective you set and each decision you make</u>.*

1. *Will I gain from reaching my objective?*
2. *What will I receive upon reaching my objective?*
3. *Will others prosper from my attainment of the objective?*
4. *Will society, Earth, and the cosmos benefit from my success in the objective?*
5. *Is my objective supported by my culture? If no, why not?*
6. *Will my objective's achievement create an overall positive energy?*
7. *Will I be happy with changes to my present situation if I meet my objective?*
8. *What must I give up to attain my objective?*
9. *What are the outcomes if I accomplish it?*
10. *What are the outcomes if I fail to achieve it?*
11. *What won't happen if I do succeed in it?*

The next step is all about designing effective goals and objectives to construct the most effective lifestyle. As you do so, refer back to the guidelines for smarter goals and ecology

Now
F-ollow O-ne C-ourse U-ntil S-uccessful

Prioritize the goals based on their significance and the mpact they will have on your life and ecology.

Break down your goals into actionable steps and determine what resources you need to achieve them.

Use the SMARTER objectives and Ecology to design your lifestyle blueprint.

Use the next exercise for discovery to define your lifestyle bjectives across various areas of life. Review the blueprint you ave designed for yourself and fill in the objectives you want to chieve within each category. Be specific and consider both hort-term and long-term goals.

Career Objectives:

1. _____

2. _____

3. _____

Family Objectives:

1. _____

2. _____

3. _____

Spiritual Objectives:

1. _____

2. _____

3. _____

Health Objectives:

1. _____

2. _____

3. _____

Fun Objectives:

1. _____

2. _____

3. _____

Community Objectives:

1. _____
2. _____
3. _____

Travel Objectives:

1. _____
2. _____
3. _____

Financial Objectives:

1. _____
2. _____
3. _____

Social Objectives:

1. _____
2. _____
3. _____

Education Objectives:

1. _____

2. _____

3. _____

Note: Once you have filled in the objectives for each category, prioritize them based on their importance and create an action plan to work towards achieving them.

Regularly review and update your objectives as needed to stay aligned with your desired lifestyle.

DO YOUR OBJECTIVES EACH COMPLY WITH THE SMARTER PROTOCOL AND ECOLOGY?

In this Chapter, we audited our current lifestyle and beliefs, forecasted our future by creating a compelling vision, and delved into our core values and overall satisfaction in life.

Now, equipped with this newfound clarity, we are ready to venture into the next chapter.

Just as a skilled mason constructs a sturdy building, each belief we embrace becomes a solid brick in the structure of our chosen lifestyle, reinforcing our commitment to living authentically and pursuing our aspirations.

3.

CONSTRUCTION

O nce you become aware of your own programming and conditioning, **you have the power to construct any kind of life you choose**.

By recognizing your own limiting beliefs and negative mental programs in chapter 2, you can now actively choose to replace them with positive beliefs that serve your life of purpose.

This chapter involves constructing your ideal lifestyle, which includes a keystone belief that anchors your worldview, foundational beliefs that support your keystone belief, and a moral code of conduct that can guide your actions with a bolster of confidence.

With these components in place, you have the freedom to pick and choose the beliefs and mental programs that will help you achieve your goals and live the life you truly desire.

It may take time and effort to reprogram your mind and build a lifestyle that aligns with your values, but the rewards of living a purposeful life are immeasurable. Remember, you have the power to create the life you want – all it takes is the courage to start

Here you have the power to construct and design a life that aligns with your values, passions, and dreams.

1. **ESTABLISH A KEYSTONE BELIEF**
2. **LAY A FOUNDATION OF HEALTHY PRESUPPOSITIONS**
3. **CREATE A MORAL CODE OF CONDUCT**
4. **REPROGRAM**

1.*Creating a keystone belief is a crucial step* in designing your ideal lifestyle. In a building a keystone is the stone that locks all others into place. This is the core belief that anchors your thoughts, actions, and decisions. It should reflect your deepest values and guide you towards your goals. When you have a clear keystone belief, you have a foundation upon which to build the rest of your beliefs and behaviors.

2. *Foundational beliefs are the building blocks* around your keystone belief. They help you define your worldview, your priorities, and your sense of purpose. By examining your foundational beliefs, you can determine what truly matters to you and what you want to achieve in life.

3. *A moral code of conduct is a set of principles that guide your behavior and decision-making.* It is a framework for ethical living that reflects your values and beliefs. By creating a moral code of conduct, you establish a clear set of standards for yourself and hold yourself accountable to them. This can help you live with integrity and build stronger relationships with others.

By combining a keystone belief, foundational beliefs, and a moral code of conduct, you can create a lifestyle that is true to who you are, supports your well-being, and brings you sustainable happiness. **You will also learn how to make and use affirmations** as a tool for reprogramming our subconsciou mind and the R.A.S. We learned about in *Chapter 2*

WITH THESE COMPONENTS IN PLACE, YOU HAVE THE FREEDOM TO PICK AND CHOOSE THE BELIEFS AND MENTAL PROGRAMS THAT WILL HELP YOU ACHIEVE YOUR GOALS AND LIVE THE LIFE YOU TRULY DESIRE.

This chapter will provide you with practical tools and exercises to help you use these key elements, so you can begin to construct a lifestyle that aligns with your values and goals.

Whether you're starting from scratch or looking to make some meaningful changes in your existing lifestyle, this chapte will provide you with the tools, strategies, and insights you need to construct a life that truly reflects who you are and wha you value.

KEYSTONE BELIEF

The first step is to identify the belief that will serve as the foundation for other beliefs.

This belief should be positive, empowering, and align with personal values and goals. Once the belief is identified, it is essential to reinforce it through repetition and positive self-talk.

Visualizing and affirming the belief regularly can help to embed it into the subconscious mind. It is also crucial to surround oneself with people, environments, and information that support this belief.

Over time, this belief will become ingrained, leading to a more positive outlook on life and attracting experiences that align with the belief.

It is important to remember that creating a keystone belief requires patience, consistency, and a willingness to challenge and replace limiting beliefs.

"ALL SUBSEQUENT BELIEFS WILL ENRICH MY LIFE, MAKE THINGS PLEASANT AND CREATE OPPORTUNITY FOR SUSTAINABLE GROWTH AND HAPPINESS. "

Making and holding a keystone belief such as the one above requires a deliberate and consistent effort. *With Keystone in place*, now lets build an unshakable foundation

FOUNDATIONAL BELIEFS/ PRESUPPOSITIONS

Without a solid foundation for your new lifestyle, each decision you make is more like playing a game of Jenga.

If we don't stand for something we can fall for everything

Foundational beliefs or *Lifestyle Architecture presuppositions* are the underlying understandings, values, or principles that we hold to be true and that shape our thinking, attitudes, and behaviors.

They are often deeply ingrained and may operate at an unconscious level, guiding our perceptions and interpretations of the world around us.

These beliefs can be beneficial by providing a stable foundation for our worldview, *helping us make sense of our experiences and guiding us in decision-making*. They can also be negative when they are rigid and inflexible, leading to dogmatic thinking and preventing us from considering alternative perspectives or adapting to new information.

In some cases, these beliefs may also be limiting and create self-imposed barriers to personal growth and development.

It is important to critically examine our foundational beliefs to ensure that they are aligned with our goals and values and are serving us in a positive way.

IT'S ALL YOUR CHOICE - ACCOUNTABILITY

At the core of our existence lies the power of choice. Every day, we make countless decisions that determine the trajectory of our lives. From the simplest choices, such as what to eat for breakfast, to the more complex ones, such as which career path to pursue, we are the architects of our own lives. Ultimately, it is our choices that shape our experiences and determine the outcomes we achieve.

However, with great power comes great responsibility. We must be willing to take accountability for the choices we make, both good and bad. ***Accepting responsibility means acknowledging that we have control over our decisions and the outcomes that follow.*** It means owning up to our mistakes, learning from them, and moving forward with renewed purpose and clarity.

It is important to recognize that although we cannot control everything outside of ourselves, we can control the way we think and perceive an experience. We have the power to choose our thoughts and reactions in any given situation, even in the face of adversity. We can choose to see challenges as opportunities for growth, and setbacks as temporary roadblocks on the path to success.

One way to learn how to take accountability is through lifestyle architecture education. This type of education helps individuals design and build their ideal life by taking a holistic approach to personal development. It teaches people how to set objectives, make intentional choices, and create healthy habits that align with their values and aspirations.

Through lifestyle architecture education, individuals can learn how to take control of their lives and make choices that lead to a fulfilling and purposeful existence. By taking accountability for their choices, they can create a life that is authentic, meaningful, and true to who they are.

NOTHING OUTSIDE YOU CONTROLS HOW YOU RESPOND

NO MAGIC PILL

There is no such thing as a magic pill that can instantly grant sustainable happiness.

While there are certainly tools and techniques that can help people cultivate happiness, it's important to recognize that true and lasting happiness requires effort and a commitment to personal growth.

Simply popping a pill or trying a new fad is unlikely to lead to sustainable happiness. Instead, it requires building healthy habits, cultivating positive relationships, developing a sense of purpose and meaning, and finding ways to manage stress and adversity.

YOU WILL NOT SOLVE YOUR PROBLEMS BY USING THE KIND OF THINKING THAT BROUGHT YOU TO THE PROBLEM.

It is often said that the definition of insanity is doing the same thing over and over again and expecting different results

Similarly, it is unlikely that we will solve our problems by using the same kind of thinking that brought us to those problems in the first place. If we want to overcome the challenges we face, we need to think outside the box and be willing to explore new perspectives and approaches. This may require us to challenge our assumptions, question our beliefs, and embrace uncertainty.

Ultimately, it is only by breaking free from our habitual ways of thinking that we can open up new possibilities and find innovative solutions to the complex problems that we face as individuals and as a society.

> In recognizing and critically evaluating our foundational beliefs and presuppositions, we empower ourselves to align our thoughts and actions with our true values and objectives. By avoiding rigid and dogmatic thinking, we open ourselves to new perspectives and growth opportunities.
>
> The presuppositions of accountability, the acknowledgment that there's no magic solution, the understanding that change requires a shift in thinking, and the realization that we control our responses, all serve as guides in this endeavor. Embracing these principles allows us to navigate the complexities of life with greater wisdom and resilience, fostering a more meaningful and fulfilling journey.

MORAL CODE OF CONDUCT

Living a fulfilling and purposeful life often requires a solid foundation and a clear direction. This is where a moral code of conduct can be invaluable.

By providing a set of values and principles to guide our decisions, a moral code acts as a compass that helps us navigate the complexities of life with greater clarity and confidence.

One of the most important aspects of a moral code is that it can **serve as an anchor of stability**. In a world that can often be unpredictable and uncertain, having a clear set of principles to fall back on can be immensely comforting. Knowing that we have **a moral compass to guide us** can help us feel more grounded and centered, even in the face of challenges and adversity.

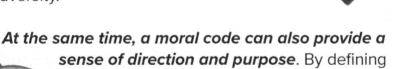

At the same time, a moral code can also provide a sense of direction and purpose. By defining what is important to us and what we stand for, our moral code can help us make decisions that align with our deepest values and goals. This can give us a sense of meaning and fulfillment, and help us live a life that feels true to who we are.

There are many possible values and principles that can be included in a moral code of conduct, some examples include kindness, gratitude, not taking things personally, not assuming, always doing your best, and the golden rule of treating others like you would like to be treated.

Kindness,

for example, can be a powerful guiding principle in all of our interactions with others. By prioritizing kindness, we can foster stronger relationships, build trust and understanding, and create a more positive and supportive environment for everyone around us.

Gratitude

Gratitude is another important value that can help us cultivate a more positive and optimistic outlook on life. By focusing on the good things in our lives and expressing gratitude for them, we can cultivate a sense of abundance and contentment that can help us weather difficult times with greater resilience and grace.

Not taking things personally and not assuming

These can also be valuable principles to guide our interactions with others. By recognizing that other people's behavior is often a reflection of their own thoughts, feelings, and experiences, rather than a direct commentary on us, we can avoid taking things too personally or making assumptions that may not be accurate.

Always doing your best

Doing your best can help us cultivate a sense of personal responsibility and accountability. By striving to do our best in everything we do, we can build a sense of pride and accomplishment that can help us feel more confident and self-assured.

The golden rule of treating others like you would like to be treated

is a universal principle that can help us navigate all of our interactions with others. By treating others with kindness, respect, and empathy, we can create a more positive and harmonious world that benefits everyone.

By providing a set of values and principles to guide our decisions, a moral code can act as a compass that helps us navigate the complexities of life with greater clarity and confidence, while also providing a sense of stability and direction.

Being impeccable with your word

is a concept that emphasizes the power and responsibility of language in our lives. It means speaking with integrity and avoiding language that harms or poisons others. It also involves being truthful, honest, and transparent in our communication. When we are impeccable with our word, we are conscious of the impact that our language can have on others, and we take care to ensure that our words are uplifting and empowering.

In addition to speaking with integrity, being impeccable with your word also means having appropriate boundaries and not agreeing to things when your plate is already full.

Many of us were told "no don't" and "stop" so much when we were younger that we never learned how to use the word "no" in a healthy way to create boundaries later in life. By setting appropriate boundaries and not overcommitting ourselves, we can avoid becoming overwhelmed and stressed, and we can maintain our integrity and authenticity in our communication with others.

Overall, being impeccable with your word involves using language as a tool for positive communication and personal growth. It means being honest and truthful with ourselves and others, respecting boundaries, and using language to uplift and empower those around us.

Quality over quantity

When it comes to achieving life satisfaction, one important aspect to consider is the quality of our life experiences. In our modern society, we are often bombarded with messages that encourage us to pursue quantity over quality - more things, more experiences, more achievements. However, this approach can often leave us feeling unfulfilled and unsatisfied, as we find ourselves constantly chasing after the next thing without taking the time to truly savor and appreciate what we already have.

Instead, we should focus on seeking out high-quality experiences that truly enrich our lives. This might mean taking the time to cultivate deep and meaningful relationships with loved ones, pursuing hobbies and interests that bring us joy and fulfillment, or simply slowing down and savoring the small moments of beauty and joy that can be found in everyday life.

By prioritizing quality over quantity, we can create a life that is rich in meaning and purpose, and that brings us genuine satisfaction and happiness. Rather than constantly striving for more, we can learn to appreciate and savor the richness of the experiences we already have, and cultivate a sense of deep contentment that will sustain us for years to come.

Slow is the fast way

When it comes to constructing a fulfilling and sustainable lifestyle, it's essential to establish foundational beliefs that guide our actions and decisions. One such belief is that "slow is the fast way." This principle reminds us that taking the time to plan and execute our goals thoughtfully and deliberately can actually save us time, energy, and resources in the long run.

For example, imagine a person who rushes through a workout without properly warming up or using proper form. They may think they're saving time by skipping steps, but in reality, they're putting themselves at risk of injury. This injury could set them back weeks or even months in their fitness journey, ultimately wasting more time than they saved by rushing.

Likewise, taking shortcuts or rushing through tasks can lead to errors and mistakes that require us to repeat the work, further delaying our progress. It's much better to take the time to do things right the first time and avoid the frustration and wasted effort that come with having to redo our work.

Finally, the belief that "slow is the fast way" encourages us to avoid assumptions and shortcuts that may seem tempting but ultimately lead to dead ends. Instead, we should take the time to research and plan our actions carefully, ensuring that we're pursuing goals that are truly meaningful to us and that we have a solid plan in place to achieve them.

By embracing the principle that "slow is the fast way," we can cultivate a lifestyle that is intentional, purposeful, and sustainable in the long term.

REPROGRAMMING

Now let's explore the powerful concept of reprogramming your subconscious mind. Just as a computer programmer writes lines of code to create software, we will utilize affirmations as the "code" to reshape our beliefs and actions, ultimately leading to a healthier and more fulfilling lifestyle.

By consciously crafting and using affirmations, we can recondition our subconscious mind, breaking free from limiting beliefs and creating new empowering habits.

REPROGRAMMING PROTOCOL

To effectively reprogram your subconscious, we will follow a protocol built upon the foundational principles of the 8 P's of programming. These guidelines will enable us to create affirmations or "codes" that are powerful agents of transformation. Let's explore each of the 8 P's and understand their significance in our journey of reprogramming the subconscious:

1. **Present**: Affirmations must be crafted in the present tense, as if the desired change has already occurred. By doing so, we align our subconscious mind with the desired outcome, making it more receptive to change.

2. **Personal**: Your affirmations should be personal and specific to your own desires and aspirations. Tailor them to resonate deeply with your individuality, making them relevant and meaningful. Do not compare yourself to someone else or what they have.

3. **Precise**: The language of your affirmations should be precise and clear, leaving no room for ambiguity. Specificity enhances the effectiveness of the affirmation and directs your subconscious mind toward the desired outcome.

4. **Positive**: Affirmations must always be framed in a positive manner. Focus on what you want to manifest, rather than what you want to avoid or eliminate. Positive affirmations empower and inspire change.

5. **Possible**: It is crucial to frame your affirmations in a way that your subconscious mind perceives as achievable. While it is essential to stretch your limits, creating affirmations that feel attainable increases the likelihood of success.

6. **Persuasive**: Craft affirmations that resonate with you on an emotional level. They should evoke strong feelings of belief and conviction, inspiring you to take action and reinforcing your commitment to change.

7. **Private**: Keep your affirmations private, at least in the initial stages. This allows you to form a personal connection with them, avoiding external judgments or skepticism that may hinder your progress.

8. **Powerful**: Your affirmations should carry a sense of power and potency. Choose words that ignite your passion and conviction, creating a deep impact on your subconscious mind.

Reprogramming your subconscious mind through affirmations is a profound exercise that holds the potential to reshape your life. By becoming conscious of our thoughts, emotions, and behaviors, we can identify when and where to utilize our affirmations most effectively.

It's vital to recognize that lifestyle architecture is a holistic process. ***Affirmations alone cannot bring about lasting change if other aspects of our lives remain neglected. We must strive for a comprehensive approach, exploring both internal and external factors that influence our well-being.***

CHOOSE YOUR OWN ADVENTURE

Through the identification of our keystone belief, the establishment of foundational beliefs, and the creation of a moral code of conduct, we have erected the framework that will guide us toward our desired existence. By becoming more aware of our values, priorities, and goals, we have equipped ourselves with the tools necessary to navigate the intricate pathways of life and to seek ultimate satisfaction.

It is crucial to recognize that our beliefs and moral code of conduct are deeply personal, shaped by our unique experiences, perspectives, and aspirations. While the suggestions presented in this chapter have served as a valuable guide, it is essential to acknowledge that they are not absolute truths.

Each individual possesses the autonomy to omit, enhance, or utilize these suggestions according to their own circumstances and beliefs. Our journey of lifestyle architecture is a deeply personal one, and we have the power to shape it in ways that align with our individuality and authenticity.

As we close this chapter and reflect upon the construction of our lifestyle, it is important to acknowledge that our blueprint is not a static entity.

In the next chapter, we will embark on an appraisal of our life, evaluating its congruence with the blueprint and the lifestyle we consciously chose to construct.

4.

CONGRUENCE APPRAISAL

Appraisal is an essential aspect of lifestyle architecture self-discovery as it helps us evaluate if our actions and decisions are aligned with our desired outcomes. This appraisal will involve an exploration of the four pillars of our lifestyle:

> **1. CHORUS OR LANGUAGE**
> **2. CASH**
> **3. COMPANY**
> **4. CONDITION**

▶ *Chorus*, or the language we use to communicate with ourselves and others

▶ *Cash*, referring to our financial well-being and the relationship we have with money

▶ *Company*, encompassing the people we surround ourselves with and the impact they have on our journey

▶ *Condition*, representing the state of our physical, mental, and emotional well-being.

By examining these pillars, we will gain valuable insights into the areas of our lives that require attention, refinement, or celebration.

When our actions are congruent with our goals, we experience a smooth ride on the road of life. However, when there is a misalignment, we encounter obstacles and challenges that make the journey rough.

Recognizing and addressing these discrepancies is crucial to achieving our desired outcomes and living a fulfilling life.

Continuously monitor and evaluate your progress towards your goals. This will help you identify any areas that need improvement and make necessary adjustments to your blueprint.

For a week analyze your daily routine, diet, exercise, sleep patterns, stress levels, and social interactions. Identify any patterns or habits that are hindering your progress towards your goals. Consider your daily routines, habits, relationships, and the environment you live in.

Are You Living a Life "on the level and true"? This Chapter will guide you to your confirmation

CHORUS / LANGUAGE

Our words have the power to shape our reality, especially when it comes to our personal growth and self-discovery. What we say to ourselves and others can either support or hinder our efforts to align with our lifestyle blueprint.

Our internal chorus, the constant chatter in our minds, has a profound impact on our emotions, thoughts, and actions. Using definitives like "always" and "never" can be dangerous in communication because they limit our options and create a sense of permanence.

It's better to use language that is solution-focused and positive, such as saying "please color on the paper" instead of "don't color on the wall." This type of wording programs our reticular alarm system to focus on what we want instead of what we don't want.

Watch your _Thoughts_, for they become words.
Watch your _Words_, for they become actions.
Watch your _Actions_, for they become habit.
Watch your _Habits_, for they become your character.
Watch your _Character_, for it becomes your
Destiny

An example from neurolinguistic programming is how the language we use can direct our behaviors and ultimately our habits. By changing our internal dialogue and external communication, we can create a more supportive environment for personal growth and self-discovery.

A checklist to evaluate if you are using the right words that are in alignment with your lifestyle blueprint:

1. *Is the word kind?*

2. *Is the word necessary?*

3. *Is the word true?*

4. *Does the word expand or contract my thinking and the thinking of those around me?*

5. *Does the word convey an optimistic or pessimistic attitude?*

6. *Is the word supportive or harmful to others or myself?*

If you answer "yes" to questions 1, 2, and 3, and "expand," "optimistic," and "supportive" to questions 4, 5, and 6, then you are on the right track with your words. If you answer "no" to any of these questions, then it might be time to re-evaluate the words you use and the impact they have on yourself and others.

Remember, this mantra...

"IF IT IS NOT KIND <u>AND</u> NECESSARY <u>AND</u> TRUE, WE SHOULD "<u>S.T.F.U.</u>"

or *"**keep our mouths shut**" in others words.* This can help you to filter out negative or harmful words, and choose to use words that are kind, necessary, and true, and that uplift and inspire others.

DON'T LET YOUR WORD<u>S</u> AND TONE<u>S</u> ACT LIKE <u>S</u>WORD AND <u>S</u>TONE

COMPANY

The company we keep can be a powerful reflection of how closely we are living in accordance with our lifestyle blueprint.

Our friends, family, and acquaintances can either uplift us and inspire us to reach our potential, or hold us back and keep us stuck in unhealthy patterns.

One way to determine whether our company is congruent with our values and goals is to look for the qualities of **compassion, competence, communication, and consistency.** When our friends and acquaintances show compassion towards us and others, demonstrate competence in their fields, communicate effectively, and exhibit consistency in their actions and values, it is a good indicator that we are surrounded by people who share our vision for a fulfilling and meaningful life.

By being mindful of the company we keep, we can create a supportive and nurturing environment that helps us to stay aligned with our true selves and live in congruence with our unique lifestyle blueprint.

A small assessment checklist to evaluate if the company of people we are keeping is beneficial for lifestyle design success, based on **competence, compassion, communication, and consistency:**

1. **Competence:**

▶ *Do the people in your company have skills, knowledge, and experience that align with your goals?*

▶ *Are they able to provide useful advice, insights, or resources that can help you achieve your lifestyle design goals?*

2. **Compassion:**

▶ *Are the people in your company supportive of your aspirations and goals?*

▶ *Do they show empathy, understanding, and kindness when you face challenges or setbacks?*

▶ *Are they able to offer constructive feedback without being overly critical or judgmental?*

3. **Communication:**

▶ *Do the people in your company communicate effectively and clearly?*

▶ *Are they willing to listen to your ideas and thoughts?*

▶ *Do they provide constructive feedback in a timely and respectful manner?*

4. Consistency:

▶ *Are the people in your company reliable and consistent in their behavior and actions?*

▶ *Do they follow through on their commitments and promises?*

▶ *Do they show up when they say they will and keep their word?*

By assessing the people in your company based on these four criteria, you can determine whether they are helping or hindering your efforts to design a successful lifestyle.

IF YOU FIND THAT CERTAIN INDIVIDUALS ARE NOT MEETING THESE STANDARDS, IT MAY BE WORTH REEVALUATING THE RELATIONSHIP OR FINDING NEW PEOPLE TO ADD TO YOUR COMPANY WHO ARE MORE ALIGNED WITH YOUR GOALS.

IF AN INDIVIDUAL HAS ALL FOUR TRAITS, YOU CAN ENJOY A HEALTHY SENSE OF CONFIDENCE AND TRUST IN THEM.

CASH

It's an essential component of modern life and plays a significant role in determining the lifestyle we lead. The way we use our cash and money can reflect whether we are living a life in alignment with our lifestyle blueprint.

Our perspective towards money can either be one of scarcity or abundance. When we operate from a scarcity mindset, we tend to view money as a limited resource and often have a fear of not having enough. This mindset can lead us to make decisions that don't align with our lifestyle goals, such as settling for a job we don't enjoy or sacrificing our passions to maintain financial stability.

In contrast, an abundance mindset allows us to see money as a renewable resource that can help us achieve our desired lifestyle. By operating from this mindset, we can make choices that align with our lifestyle blueprint and bring us closer to the life we envision.

Our relationship with money reflects our perspective towards scarcity and abundance, and it can be a valuable tool to guide us towards living a congruent lifestyle.

Here some things to consider when evaluating whether you are using your cash or money in a way that aligns with your lifestyle blueprint:

1. Have you created a budget or financial plan that aligns with your lifestyle goals and priorities?

2. Are you tracking your spending regularly to ensure that you are staying within your budget?

3. Are you saving enough money for your short-term and long-term goals, such as emergencies, vacations, retirement, or investments?

4. Are you avoiding unnecessary expenses that do not align with your values or priorities?

5. Are you investing in yourself by paying for education, health, or personal development that aligns with your goals and values?

6. Are you giving back to your community or supporting causes that align with your values and passions?

7. Are you avoiding debt or managing your debt in a way that is sustainable and aligned with your financial plan?

8. Are you reviewing and adjusting your financial plan regularly to ensure that it reflects your changing goals and priorities?

By answering these questions honestly, you can identify areas where you may need to adjust your financial habits to better align with your lifestyle blueprint.

CONDITION

In the pursuit of self-discovery and life satisfaction, one's mental and physical health should not be overlooked.

Our bodies are a reflection of our lifestyles and the choices we make, and understanding this connection can provide valuable insights into our overall well-being.

Are you Stressed?

It's important to note that this checklist serves as a general guideline, and experiencing a few of these signs doesn't necessarily indicate negative stress.

However, You cannot just wish stress away, *if you find yourself consistently experiencing several of these symptoms, objectively you are stressed. it may be helpful to seek support from a healthcare professional or explore stress management techniques to address the issue.*

Check the ones you experience frequently

Physical Symptoms:

☐ *Increased heart rate or palpitations*
☐ *Frequent headaches or migraines*
☐ *Muscle tension or body aches*
☐ *Digestive issues (e.g., stomachaches, diarrhea)*
☐ *Changes in appetite (overeating or loss of appetite)*
☐ *Sleep disturbances (insomnia or excessive sleep)*

Emotional and Behavioral Signs:

☐ *Feeling overwhelmed or constantly worried*
☐ *Irritability or quick temper*
☐ *Difficulty concentrating or making decisions*
☐ *Racing thoughts or inability to relax*
☐ *Increased use of substances (e.g., alcohol, drugs)*
☐ *Withdrawal from social activities or relationships*
☐ *Procrastination or avoidance of responsibilities*

Cognitive Indicators:

☐ *Persistent negative thoughts or pessimism*
☐ *Inability to focus or racing mind*
☐ *Forgetfulness or decreased memory recall*
☐ *Lack of motivation or decreased productivity*
☐ *Difficulty in problem-solving or decision-making*
☐ *Reduced creativity or impaired judgment*

Lifestyle Changes:

☐ Neglected self-care activities (e.g., exercise, healthy eating)
☐ Increased reliance on caffeine, nicotine, or other stimulants
☐ Disturbed work-life balance or long working hours
☐ Decreased interest in hobbies or leisure activities
☐ Neglected personal relationships or social engagements
☐ Poor time management or constant feeling of being rushed

Emotional Well-being:

☐ Frequent feelings of anxiety, panic, or restlessness
☐ Feelings of sadness, hopelessness, or helplessness
☐ Reduced self-esteem or feelings of worthlessness
☐ Loss of interest or pleasure in previously enjoyed activities
☐ Difficulty experiencing positive emotions
☐ Frequent mood swings or emotional instability

Interpersonal Relationships:

☐ Increased conflicts or arguments with loved ones
☐ Difficulty in expressing emotions or communicating effectively
☐ Isolation or social withdrawal
☐ Strained relationships with colleagues or superiors
☐ Lack of support from friends or family members
☐ Feelings of loneliness or disconnectedness

5.
MAINTENANCE

Maintaining a purposeful, free, and sustainable happy lifestyle requires constant attention and effort. In this chapter on maintenance, we will focus on critical aspects of sustainable living - energy resource management, motivation, essential self-care.

1. ENERGY RESOURCE MANAGEMENT
2. MOTIVATION
3. 5 ESSENTIAL ENHANCEMENTS

First, we will examine **how we waste energy** and identify ways to conserve it through efficient practices. We will also explore how we can invest our energy wisely in activities that align with our values and purpose.

Second, we will check out the **science of motivation** and explore how we can boost our feel-good chemicals such as dopamine, oxytocin, serotonin and endorphins.

Finally, we will discuss **five essential enhancements** that can help us stay on track, including cultivating an optimistic attitude, staying hydrated, focusing on nutrition instead of dieting, engaging in playful activities instead of just exercise, and incorporating body treatments like massage, acupressure, and reflexology.

By adopting these practices, we can design a lifestyle that sustains our well-being, purpose, and happiness.

LIFESTYLE ARCHITECTURE IS AN ONGOING PROCESS THAT REQUIRES CONSISTENT CARE AND DEDICATION. IT'S ESSENTIAL TO MAINTAIN YOUR LIFESTYLE BY STAYING COMMITTED TO YOUR OBJECTIVES AND VALUES.

Celebrate your achievements and continue to make adjustments as needed to keep your blueprint relevant and effective.

ENERGY RESOURCE MANAGEMENT

I n the pursuit of a lifestyle that promotes freedom and sustainable happiness, the management of our energy resources is of utmost importance. Our energy is a precious commodity, and how we utilize it has a direct impact on our overall well-being. In fact, the way we use our energy can be categorized into three distinct categories: *waste, conserve, and invest.*

WASTE

When we waste energy, we use it in ways that do not serve us or our goals or health. There are several ways in which we can waste our energy, but 5 of the most common include negative triggers, not being present, codependency, procrastination, and lack of efficiency.

1. **Negative triggers:**

Such as ***fear, anger, and worry*** can cause us to expend a tremendous amount of energy. These emotions can be draining and can leave us feeling exhausted, irritable, and unmotivated. When we allow these emotions to consume us, we waste valuable energy that could be better spent on more positive pursuits.

2. Presence:

Similarly, **not being present in the moment** can also be a major source of energy waste. When we dwell on past events or worry about future tribulations, we use up our energy on things that are beyond our control. This can leave us feeling anxious and overwhelmed, and it can also prevent us from fully engaging with the present moment.

3. Codependency:

Finally, **codependency** can also be a significant drain on our energy resources. When we rely on others for our happiness and well-being, we give away our power and agency. This can leave us feeling helpless and dependent, and it can also lead to feelings of resentment and frustration.

4. Inefficiency:

In regards to self-discovery and lifestyle architecture, understanding the importance of efficient energy resource management is paramount.

Just as a poorly insulated home leaks heat, the lack of efficiency in our daily lives can result in wasted energy. When we fail to optimize our time, resources, and habits, we unwittingly squander the precious energy needed to propel us towards a life of purpose, freedom, and sustainable happiness.

Whether it be through disorganized schedules, ineffective decision-making, or neglecting our physical and emotional well-being, inefficient practices drain us of the vital fuel we need to pursue our passions and live with intention.

Recognizing this, we must actively seek ways to streamline our routines, align our actions with our values, and cultivate sustainable habits that replenish our energy reserves rather than deplete them. By embracing efficiency, we unlock the potential for a more focused, fulfilling, and vibrant existence, where every ounce of energy is channeled towards building the life we envision.

5. Procrastination:

In the realm of energy resource management, procrastination and prolonged resolution can be formidable foes that drain our vitality and cast a shadow over the enjoyment of life.

When we continually put off important tasks or decisions, we squander precious energy that could otherwise be directed towards pursuing our passions and cultivating a life of purpose.

Procrastination creates a cloud of unfinished business hanging over our heads, constantly reminding us of the tasks left undone and the opportunities left unexplored. This cloud obscures the sunshine of joy and fun, casting a shadow over our experiences and hindering our ability to fully immerse ourselves in the present moment.

By recognizing the detrimental impact of procrastination on our energy levels and overall well-being, we can take proactive steps to break free from its grip and reclaim our zest for life.

CONSERVATION

On the other hand, **when we conserve our energy,** we use it in ways that support our well-being and goals. This means being intentional about how we use our energy and avoiding unnecessary drains on our resources.

Our energy, both physical and mental, is finite, and learning to conserve and channel it wisely is key to living a fulfilling and balanced life. *Let's explore how the profound impact of certain actions and thought patterns that can help us conserve and channel our energy towards personal growth*. By implementing these practices, we can cultivate a sense of balance, clarity, and increased efficiency in our lives.

1. *Setting Clear Boundaries:*

One of the fundamental steps in energy resource management is setting clear boundaries. When we establish boundaries, we create space for ourselves, both physically and emotionally. This allows us to protect our energy from being unnecessarily depleted by external influences or draining relationships.

By learning to say "no" when it aligns with our values and priorities, we honor our own needs and preserve valuable energy for the things that truly matter. Setting boundaries also fosters a sense of self-respect and empowerment, enabling us to invest our energy wisely.

2. *Practicing Mindfulness:*

Mindfulness is a powerful tool for conserving and replenishing our energy. By practicing present-moment awareness, we cultivate a deep connection with our inner selves. This awareness helps us identify energy-draining thoughts and emotions that arise from dwelling on the past or worrying about the future.

Through mindfulness, we can redirect our attention to the present, releasing unnecessary mental burdens and conserving energy that would otherwise be wasted. Regular mindfulness practices such as meditation, deep breathing, or engaging in activities that bring us joy can create a reservoir of energy that fuels our self-discovery journey.

3. *Increasing Efficiency:*

Efficiency plays a pivotal role in energy resource management. When we optimize our actions and thought patterns, we minimize the energy required to accomplish our goals.

By embracing organization, planning, and prioritization, we can streamline our activities and avoid energy-sapping distractions. Breaking tasks into smaller, manageable steps and focusing on one thing at a time helps us to avoid feeling overwhelmed, conserving mental and emotional energy.

INVESTMENT

Just like a battery, our energy levels can be depleted or charged based on our actions and thought patterns. By consciously investing in our energy, we can increase our capacity to live life fully and authentically. Lets explore three key aspects of energy investments prioritizing self-care, strengthening the mind and spiritual refinement. These practices act as investments, allowing us to tap into a greater source of energy and strength, akin to expanding our battery's capacity.

1. *Prioritizing Self-Care:*

The first step in energy resource management is prioritizing self-care. It involves understanding the fundamental aspects of well-being and consciously nurturing them.

By incorporating the following **five essential enhancements into our lives**—positive attitude, hydration, nutrition, playful activity, and body treatments—we can recharge our energy levels and expand our capacity for a more fulfilling existence. We will discuss each later with detail in *chapter 5 maintenance*

Self-care is an essential component of energy resource management. It involves consciously attending to our physical, mental, and emotional well-being. Prioritizing self-care replenishes our energy reserves, enhances resilience, and enables us to navigate life's challenges with greater ease.

When we prioritize self-care, we honor our own needs and create a solid foundation of vitality and strength. This empowers us to engage with the world from a place of abundance rather than depletion, enabling us to give our best to others and pursue our passions with enthusiasm and vigor.

2. *Strengthen the mind:*

Engaging in mental activities is crucial for maintaining brain health and optimizing cognitive function. To keep your brain in top shape, it's essential to constantly challenge yourself by learning new things, whether it's exploring different subjects, acquiring new skills, or diving into languages or musical instruments.

Solving puzzles and playing brain games like chess, Tetris, and strategy games stimulates memory, problem-solving, and critical thinking abilities, promoting mental agility and sharpness.

Reading and writing are also powerful tools for brain health; reading enhances vocabulary, comprehension, and analytical thinking, while writing through journaling or creative endeavors fosters self-expression, clarity of thought, and memory retention.

Similar to how we take preventive measures to keep our bodies healthy, these mental activities act as a preventative medicine for our brains. They contribute to building cognitive resilience, improving memory, enhancing focus, and boosting overall cognitive function. Regularly challenging ourselves mentally can help ward off cognitive decline and age-related cognitive disorders.

3. *Spiritual Refinement: Tapping into Transcendent Energy:*

Beyond physical abilities, there exists a vast wellspring of energy that transcends the boundaries of our physical existence. Spiritual refinement is the process of connecting with this deeper source of strength and vitality. By nurturing our spirituality, we tap into a force that surpasses our limited understanding, granting us access to boundless energy reserves.

Spiritual refinement is a highly personal journey, shaped by individual beliefs and practices. It involves exploring and nurturing our innermost selves, connecting with something greater than ourselves, and finding meaning and purpose in life. Through practices such as meditation, prayer, mindfulness, or connecting with nature, we cultivate a deeper connection with our spiritual essence.

When we tap into our spiritual dimension, we become attuned to a well of energy that resides within us and connects us to the larger universe. This energy fuels our purpose, provides solace during challenging times, and unlocks strength beyond our physical capabilities. Spiritual refinement acts as an investment in our energy capacity, expanding our battery of existence to new dimensions.

The way we manage our energy resources is a crucial aspect of maintaining a lifestyle that promotes freedom and sustainable happiness.

BY _AVOIDING_ ENERGY WASTE, _CONSERVING_ OUR RESOURCES, AND _INVESTING_ IN OUR GROWTH AND WELL-BEING, WE CAN CULTIVATE A LIFE THAT IS FULFILLING, MEANINGFUL, AND SUSTAINABLE OVER THE LONG TERM.

MOTIVATION

Motivation is the driving force behind our actions, propelling us towards certain goals or away from undesirable outcomes. It serves as the engine that fuels our ambitions, aspirations, and desires.

When we embark on a journey of self-discovery and lifestyle architecture, understanding the dynamics of motivation becomes crucial.

Motivation can be categorized into **two main types:** positive motivation and negative motivation.

Positive motivation stems from a desire to attain or experience something we perceive as positive, enriching, or fulfilling. It draws us closer to what we want more of in our lives, whether it be success, happiness, love, or personal growth.

On the other hand, **negative motivation** arises from the desire to avoid or escape something we perceive as negative, unpleasant, or detrimental. It acts as a driving force that pushes us away from what we do not want to have in our lives, such as pain, failure, loneliness, or stagnation. Both positive and negative motivations play significant roles in shaping our actions and decisions.

HOWEVER, WHEN WE LOOK DEEPER INTO THE NATURE OF MOTIVATION, WE COME TO REALIZE THAT WHAT WE PERCEIVE AS OUR DRIVING FORCES ARE, IN FACT, INTRICATELY LINKED TO THE INTRICATE WORKINGS OF OUR BODY'S HORMONES AND NEUROTRANSMITTERS.

These chemical messengers within us orchestrate a complex symphony that influences our thoughts, emotions, and behaviors.

In our evolutionary past, these hormones and neurotransmitters primarily served the purpose of ensuring our survival. They were released in response to primal needs such as hunger, thirst, and reproduction, pushing us to seek out necessary resources and procreate to ensure the continuation of our species.

Yet, in the modern world we inhabit, where immediate life survival is not a typical concern for many, these biological mechanisms manifest in a multitude of ways beyond basic survival instincts. We engage in activities that bring us pleasure, fulfillment, and a sense of connection with others.

However, not all avenues we explore for emotional gratification are beneficial or productive. Some behaviors can be harmful, such as addiction to intoxicants, which hijack our brain's reward circuitry and lead to detrimental consequences in our lives. Similarly, certain activities, like indulging in endless hours of phone games like Candy Crush, can consume valuable time and hinder our personal growth.

To navigate the landscape of motivation effectively, it is vital to understand the underlying mechanisms that drive our desires and actions. By developing this awareness, we can discern between motivations that align with our long-term well-being and those that distract us or impede our progress.

Dopamine

Focus on the healthier ways to boost dopamine levels, such as pursuing meaningful goals, engaging in hobbies and creative activities, practicing regular play, and fostering positive social connections.

Oxytocin

Prioritize healthy ways of increasing oxytocin, such as nurturing close relationships, engaging in acts of kindness and empathy, practicing positive communication, and participating in activities that promote social bonding and emotional well-being.

Serotonin

*It's important to prioritize healthy practices to support serotonin levels, such as maintaining a balanced lifestyle, engaging in regular play, practicing stress management techniques, fostering social connections, and **seeking professional help if experiencing symptoms of depression or other mental health conditions.***

Endorphins

Dance like no one is watching, Laugh till it hurts, any playful activity you enjoy will be the safe choice to promote a natural release of endorphins

---

Most of what you do is more a condition than a thought . *DOSE* responsibly and condition your yourself to healthy choices - automatically

HOW TO STAY HIGH ON YOUR OWN SUPPLY -

The 4 happy Chemicals

In the journey of self-discovery, we often find ourselves seeking lasting motivation to pursue our dreams and live a fulfilling life. Have you ever wondered why some days you feel an unstoppable drive to conquer the world, while on other days, your motivation seems to vanish into thin air? The answer lies within the intricate chemistry of our brains. Motivation, it turns out, is more than just a state of mind—it is a chemical experience.

By unlocking the secrets of our own biochemistry, we can learn to "stay high on our own supply" and maintain a enduring state of motivation. This can be achieved through adopting healthy habits that allow us to alter our brain chemistry and release the four main happy chemicals in a natural, sustainable manner.

In this section, we will explore each of these happy chemicals and discover practical ways to stimulate their release. By integrating these strategies into our daily lives, we can create a positive feedback loop that fuels our motivation, enhances our well-being, and propels us towards a life of fulfillment.

Let's jump into the incredible world of our brain's chemistry and uncover the keys to sustaining our own happiness through self-designed lifestyle architecture. Here we will learn how to **DOSE** naturally from the inside - out.

DOPAMINE - REWARD

Dopamine represents the pleasant sensation that a reward awaits.
It serves as your brain's indicator that a requirement is about to be fulfilled. Dopamine fills you with exhilaration when you achieve a goal or acquire a prized possession.

Here are some natural and everyday activities that can help release dopamine, often referred to as the "reward hormone":

1. ***Set and Achieve Goals:*** Setting meaningful goals and working towards them can provide a sense of accomplishment and satisfaction, triggering the release of dopamine. Break down larger goals into smaller, achievable tasks to experience a continuous dopamine boost as you make progress.

2. ***Playful Activity:*** Engaging in regular exercise and physical activity, such as jogging, swimming, or playing a sport, can increase dopamine levels. Aim for activities that you enjoy and that get your heart rate up to experience the energizing effects of dopamine.

3. **Try Something New:** Exploring new experiences, hobbies, or learning a new skill can activate the release of dopamine. It could be trying a new recipe, learning to play a musical instrument, or taking up a creative endeavor. The novelty and challenge associated with new activities can be rewarding and boost dopamine levels.

4. **Practice Mindfulness and Meditation:** Engaging in mindfulness practices, such as meditation or deep breathing exercises, can increase dopamine levels. Mindfulness helps to focus your attention, reduce stress, and promote a sense of calm and contentment.

5. **Listen to Music:** Listening to music you enjoy, especially if it's upbeat or has a personal meaning to you, can trigger the release of dopamine. Create playlists of your favorite songs and use music as a tool to enhance your mood and motivation.

6. **Socialize and Connect:** Spending time with friends, family, or loved ones and engaging in meaningful social interactions can elevate dopamine levels. Building and nurturing positive relationships can provide a sense of connection and reward.

7. **Practice Small Acts of Self-Care:** Engaging in self-care activities, such as taking breaks, practicing relaxation techniques, or indulging in activities that bring you joy, can boost dopamine levels. Prioritize self-care to recharge and reward yourself.

Dopamine is a neurotransmitter associated with pleasure, reward, motivation, and reinforcement. While increasing dopamine levels can be beneficial for motivation and enjoyment, certain behaviors aimed at boosting dopamine release can have harmful side effects. Here are some examples:

1. **Substance Abuse:** Drugs such as cocaine, amphetamines, and opioids can cause a surge in dopamine levels, leading to intense euphoria. However, these substances can be highly addictive and have severe short-term and long-term health consequences, including addiction, neurological damage, and mental health disorders.

2. **Gambling and Risky Behaviors:** Engaging in high-risk activities, such as gambling or extreme sports, can stimulate dopamine release due to the anticipation of potential rewards or adrenaline rushes. However, excessive gambling can lead to financial problems, addiction, and strained relationships, while risky behaviors may result in physical injuries or even death.

3. **Excessive Consumption of Junk Food:** Consuming foods high in fat, sugar, and salt can lead to a temporary dopamine surge, providing a pleasurable sensation. However, relying on these foods excessively can contribute to weight gain, metabolic disorders, and an increased risk of chronic diseases such as diabetes and heart disease.

4. ***Excessive Social Media Use:*** The constant use of social media platforms and receiving "likes" and positive feedback can trigger dopamine release. However, excessive social media consumption can lead to addictive behaviors, feelings of inadequacy, social comparison, and negatively impact mental health, including increased risk of anxiety and depression.

5.***Sensation-seeking Behaviors:*** Engaging in extreme thrill-seeking activities solely for the purpose of seeking excitement and dopamine release, such as reckless driving or drug abuse, can result in serious physical harm, legal consequences, and damage to personal relationships.

OXYTOCIN - LOVE, TRUST & MORALITY

Oxytocin induces a sense of positive social trust, fostering feelings of security and connection.
The release of oxytocin occurs when individuals stay within the social group, allowing mammals to lower their defenses in the presence of trusted companions.

Through a series of experiments, Dr. Paul Zak discovered that oxytocin plays a crucial role in promoting social bonds, trust, and prosocial behaviors among humans. By investigating the release of oxytocin in response to various stimuli, such as watching emotional videos or engaging in acts of trust, he revealed the hormone's significance in human interactions, cooperation, and even economic decisions.

Here are some natural and everyday activities that can help release oxytocin, often referred to as the "love hormone":

1. **Hug and Cuddle:** Physical touch, such as hugging, cuddling, or holding hands, can stimulate the release of oxytocin. Spending quality time with loved ones and engaging in affectionate gestures can promote feelings of closeness and bonding.

2. **Pet Therapy:** Interacting with animals, particularly dogs and cats, has been shown to increase oxytocin levels. Petting, playing, or simply being in the presence of a furry friend can help induce a sense of calm and well-being

3. **Engage in Acts of Kindness:** Performing acts of kindness, whether it's helping someone in need, volunteering, or simply showing compassion, can trigger the release of oxytocin. Acts of kindness not only benefit others but also enhance your own sense of happiness and connection.

4. **Share Quality Time:** Simply spending quality time with loved ones, engaging in meaningful conversations, and building strong social connections can boost oxytocin levels. Make an effort to prioritize and nurture your relationships.

5. ***Practice Bonding Activities:*** Engage in activities that promote bonding and togetherness, such as sharing a meal, playing games, going for a walk, or engaging in a hobby with loved ones. These shared experiences can enhance feelings of trust and intimacy, leading to increased oxytocin release.

6. ***Express Gratitude and Appreciation:*** Expressing gratitude and appreciation to others can foster positive emotions and deepen social connections. Take time to acknowledge and thank the people in your life for their support and love.

7. ***Practice Self-Care:*** Engaging in self-care activities, such as taking a relaxing bath, practicing mindfulness, listening to soothing music, or indulging in a hobby you enjoy, can promote feelings of self-love and trigger the release of oxytocin.

By incorporating these activities into your daily life, you can enhance your relationships, well-being, and overall sense of connection with others.

Oxytocin is often referred to as the "love hormone" or "cuddle hormone" because it is associated with social bonding, trust, and intimacy. While increasing oxytocin levels can have positive effects on well-being, some practices aimed at boosting oxytocin release can have harmful side effects. Here are a few examples:

1. ***Unprotected Casual Sex:*** Engaging in casual sexual encounters without proper protection or with multiple partners can potentially increase oxytocin levels due to physical intimacy. However, it also carries the risk of sexually transmitted infections (STIs) and unwanted pregnancies, emphasizing the importance of responsible and safe sexual practices.

2. ***Excessive Attachment or Codependency:*** Over-reliance on others for emotional support and an excessive need for closeness can lead to unhealthy dynamics in relationships. While oxytocin is involved in building trust and connection, excessive attachment or codependency can lead to emotional dependency, lack of personal boundaries, and relationship dissatisfaction.

3. ***Substance Abuse:*** Certain drugs, such as MDMA (ecstasy), have been associated with an increase in oxytocin levels and feelings of empathy and bonding. However, these substances carry significant health risks, including addiction, neurotoxicity, and potential long-term psychological consequences.

4. ***Self-Harm or Risky Behaviors:*** Some individuals may engage in self-harm or risky behaviors as a maladaptive coping mechanism to seek comfort or connection. While these actions may temporarily increase oxytocin levels due to the release of stress hormones, they can lead to severe physical and psychological harm, and should never be encouraged or practiced.

5. *Manipulative Behavior:* Manipulating or exploiting others' emotions to elicit a desired response can lead to temporary increases in oxytocin levels. However, engaging in manipulative behavior undermines trust, damages relationships, and can have long-term negative effects on one's social connections and overall well-being.

SEROTONIN - MOOD STABILIZER

Serotonin can be described as the pleasant sensation of social empowerment. It fills you with a sense of pride when you receive respect and allows you to be authentic without the need to conceal anything. It's not about aggression; rather, it fosters a serene state of being, providing you with the inner calm and fortitude required to fulfill your needs.

Research has shown fascinating connections between posture and serotonin release in both lobsters and humans. While lobsters are known for their distinctive posturing behaviors during mating, humans also exhibit similar responses that can lead to serotonin release.

In the case of lobsters, these crustaceans engage in a complex series of posturing behaviors as part of their mating ritual. Male lobsters will raise their claws, extend their antennae, and arch their bodies in an elaborate display to attract females. This posturing behavior serves as a visual signal to indicate their readiness to mate. Intriguingly, studies have found that during this display, lobsters experience a surge in serotonin release.

Serotonin is a neurotransmitter that plays a crucial role in regulating mood, social behavior, and various physiological processes in both lobsters and humans. It is often associated with feelings of well-being, happiness, and overall positive affect. The release of serotonin in lobsters during their mating postures suggests a potential link between social signaling and serotonin modulation.

Similar dynamics can be observed in humans. Numerous studies have highlighted the profound impact of body posture on mood and psychological well-being. In particular, research has shown that adopting an upright, expansive posture can trigger an increase in serotonin levels in humans. This effect is often associated with enhanced self-confidence, reduced stress levels, and a more positive emotional state.

For example, a landmark study conducted by social psychologist Amy Cuddy and her colleagues demonstrated that assuming a "power pose," characterized by open body postures (such as standing tall with arms raised) for just a few minutes, led to an increase in testosterone (a hormone associated with dominance) and a decrease in cortisol (a stress hormone) levels.

These hormonal changes were accompanied by an elevation in serotonin levels, resulting in a more positive and confident state of mind.

The connection between posture and serotonin release in both lobsters and humans highlights the intricate interplay between body language, neurochemistry, and emotional states. While lobsters' posturing behavior is likely driven by evolutionary factors related to mating and social hierarchy within their species, humans can consciously leverage their posture to positively influence their mood and well-being.

It's important to note that **while posture can have a significant impact on serotonin release, it is not a panacea for all psychological and emotional issues.** Factors such as genetics, environment, and individual differences play substantial roles in determining serotonin levels and overall mental health.

Here are some natural and everyday activities that can help release serotonin, often referred to as the "happiness hormone":

1. *Get Exposure to Sunlight:* Spending time outdoors and getting exposure to natural sunlight can boost serotonin levels. Aim for at least 15-30 minutes of sunlight each day, especially in the morning, to enhance your mood and overall well-being.

2. ***Playful Activity Regularly:*** Engaging in regular physical activity, such as walking, jogging, or yoga, can increase serotonin levels. Aim for at least 30 minutes of moderate-intensity exercise most days of the week to experience the mood-boosting effects of serotonin. Make sure you are having fun.

3. ***Eat a Balanced Diet:*** Consuming a balanced diet that includes foods rich in tryptophan, such as turkey, salmon, eggs, nuts, and seeds, can help promote serotonin production. Additionally, including complex carbohydrates like whole grains and legumes can support the absorption of tryptophan and boost serotonin levels.

4. ***Address Posture:*** Adjusting one's posture can have a profound impact on both physiological and psychological well-being. According to research, adopting an upright and open posture, referred to as "power posing," can increase feelings of confidence and may even lead to a rise in serotonin levels, a hormone associated with feelings of happiness and relaxation. Good posture not only helps in opening up the chest area, leading to more effective breathing but also contributes to how a person presents themselves to the world. Physically, it allows a clear, unobstructed view of the surroundings, and metaphorically, it represents a stance of readiness and openness, altering one's perspective towards life. Such alignment and self-awareness encourage a more positive outlook and may foster a greater sense of control and contentment in everyday situations.

5. ***Engage in Acts of Kindness:*** Performing acts of kindness and showing compassion towards others can boost serotonin levels. Look for opportunities to help and support others, whether it's through volunteering, lending a listening ear, or offering a helping hand.

6. ***Cultivate Gratitude:*** Practicing gratitude and focusing on the positive aspects of your life can increase serotonin levels. Take time each day to reflect on things you are grateful for, whether it's writing them down in a journal or sharing them with others.

7. ***Engage in Relaxation Techniques:*** Engaging in relaxation techniques like progressive muscle relaxation, guided imagery, or aromatherapy can promote feelings of calmness and increase serotonin levels. Find techniques that work for you and incorporate them into your daily routine.

While increasing serotonin levels can have positive effects on mood and mental health, some practices aimed at boosting serotonin release can have harmful side effects. Here are a few examples:

1. ***Excessive Serotonin-Boosting Supplements:*** Some individuals may turn to over-the-counter supplements or herbal remedies that claim to increase serotonin levels. However, excessive use or incorrect dosages of these supplements can lead to serotonin syndrome, a potentially life-threatening condition characterized by agitation, confusion, rapid heartbeat, and high blood pressure.

2. ***Selective Serotonin Reuptake Inhibitors (SSRIs)
Misuse:*** SSRIs are commonly prescribed medications for
depression and anxiety disorders as they increase
serotonin levels in the brain. However, using SSRIs
without a prescription or exceeding the recommended
dosage can lead to adverse side effects, including
serotonin syndrome, sexual dysfunction, and withdrawal
symptoms.

3. ***Disruption of Sleep Patterns:*** Adequate sleep is
essential for maintaining healthy serotonin levels.
Disrupting sleep patterns, such as consistently getting
insufficient sleep or engaging in irregular sleep
schedules, can negatively impact serotonin regulation,
leading to mood disturbances, impaired cognitive
function, and increased risk of mental health disorders.

4. ***Excessive Alcohol Consumption:*** Alcohol initially
increases serotonin release, contributing to feelings of
relaxation and happiness. However, chronic and
excessive alcohol consumption can disrupt serotonin
production and regulation, leading to decreased
serotonin levels and an increased risk of developing
alcohol use disorders and depression.

5. ***Isolation and Lack of Social Support:*** Social
connections and positive social interactions are essential
for serotonin regulation. Isolation, loneliness, and a lack
of social support can lead to decreased serotonin levels
and an increased risk of mood disorders such as
depression and anxiety.

ENDORPHINS - EUPHORIA THE PAIN MASKER

Endorphins act as a shield against pain, enveloping the body in a blissful sensation. Their purpose lies in safeguarding the survival of injured mammals, facilitating their escape from imminent threats.

Endorphins are natural hormones produced by the body that are responsible for reducing pain and promoting feelings of pleasure. These chemicals are neurotransmitters that work by binding to specific receptors in the brain and nervous system. When endorphins are released, they produce a euphoric feeling, sometimes described as a "runner's high."

When our endorphin levels are not balanced or sufficient, we may experience symptoms such as fatigue, depression, and chronic pain. In severe cases, a deficiency in endorphins can lead to addiction, as individuals may seek out substances or activities that artificially increase endorphin levels. This can be harmful in the long term, as it can lead to a dependence on external sources of pleasure rather than the body's natural ability to produce endorphins.

Tattoos can boost endorphins, leading to feelings of euphoria during the process. This can make the experience therapeutic for some.

However, chasing this "high" can result in over-reliance or impulsive tattoo choices, as seeking tattoos mainly for the endorphin rush *might lead to regrets later.*

Fortunately, there are natural ways to increase endorphin levels in the body. Exercise is one of the most effective ways to boost endorphins, as physical activity stimulates the release of these hormones. Eating certain foods, such as dark chocolate, spicy foods, and foods high in protein, can also increase endorphin levels. Additionally, practicing mindfulness, meditation, and deep breathing can help reduce stress and promote the release of endorphins.

1. **Engage in deep breathing exercises:** Deep breathing helps to activate the relaxation response and can increase the release of endorphins. Take slow, deep breaths, filling your lungs completely, and exhale slowly. Focus on the sensation of the breath as it enters and leaves your body.

2. **Incorporate playful activities or dancing:** Engaging in playful activities like dancing, skipping, or playing games can stimulate the release of endorphins. Let loose and move your body in a way that feels fun and enjoyable. It doesn't have to be a formal exercise routine; the key is to be playful and have fun.

3. **Laugh heartily:** Laughter is a natural and powerful way to release endorphins. Watch a funny video, spend time with friends who make you laugh, or read a joke book. Allow yourself to fully embrace the laughter and enjoy the positive effects it has on your mood.

4. ***Enjoy a massage or self-massage:*** Massage therapy has been shown to increase endorphin levels and promote relaxation. Treat yourself to a professional massage or try self-massage techniques like using a foam roller or gently massaging your temples, neck, or shoulders to release tension and stimulate endorphin release.

5. ***Connect with nature:*** Spending time in nature has been proven to have numerous health benefits, including the release of endorphins. Take a walk in a park, go for a hike, or simply sit outside and appreciate the natural beauty around you. Breathing in fresh air and enjoying the sights and sounds of nature can have a positive impact on your well-being.

6. ***Watch, read or listen to something inspirational:*** Watching or reading something that inspires you can evoke positive emotions and trigger the release of endorphins. It could be a motivational TED Talk, an uplifting movie, or a book that fills you with a sense of hope and inspiration. Find content that resonates with you and brings joy or inspiration to your life.

7. ***Practice gratitude:*** Cultivating a mindset of gratitude can boost your mood and increase the release of endorphins. Take a few moments each day to reflect on the things you are grateful for. Write them down in a journal or simply express them in your mind. Focusing on the positive aspects of your life can help shift your perspective and enhance your overall well-being.

While seeking ways to increase endorphins is generally beneficial for mood enhancement and well-being, some practices may carry potential harmful side effects, both short-term and long-term. Here is a small list of activities that can have adverse effects:

1. ***Excessive Consumption of Junk Food:*** Eating sugary, processed foods can provide a temporary boost in endorphin levels. However, indulging in these foods too frequently can lead to weight gain, increased risk of chronic diseases, and nutritional deficiencies.

2. ***Substance Abuse:*** Certain substances, such as opioids and alcohol, can trigger the release of endorphins, producing a euphoric feeling. However, long-term substance abuse can lead to addiction, physical and mental health problems, and a host of negative consequences for overall well-being.

3. ***Overexercising:*** Engaging in intense exercise releases endorphins, often referred to as "runner's high." However, excessive exercise without proper rest and recovery can lead to physical injuries, chronic fatigue, hormone imbalances, and mental health issues like exercise addiction or body dysmorphia.

4. ***Risky Behaviors:*** Some individuals may seek thrill-seeking activities like extreme sports or dangerous stunts to experience an adrenaline rush, which can indirectly affect endorphin release. These activities, however, carry significant risks of physical injury, disability, or even death.

5. ***Self-harm:*** While self-inflicted pain triggers endorphin release as a self-soothing mechanism, deliberately causing harm to oneself is highly dangerous and can result in severe physical and psychological consequences. Self-harm is a sign of underlying emotional distress and requires professional help.

> If you are concerned about your well-being or the potential negative effects of any behavior, it is advisable to seek guidance from healthcare professionals or mental health experts.

CORTISOL - THE "STRESS" HORMONE

In the intricate architecture of our bodies, there exists a powerful hormone called cortisol that plays a significant role in our daily lives.

Cortisol, often referred to as the "stress hormone," is produced by the adrenal glands and released in response to stress or perceived threats.

While cortisol serves an essential purpose in our survival mechanism, chronic or excessive levels can have detrimental effects on our overall well-being.

The Role of Cortisol

When faced with a stressful situation, cortisol helps prepare our bodies to respond effectively. It increases alertness, enhances focus, and mobilizes energy reserves, enabling us to face challenges head-on. Cortisol triggers the release of glucose into the bloodstream, providing quick energy to the muscles and brain. Additionally, it regulates various bodily functions, including metabolism, blood pressure, and immune response.

Cortisol Imbalance: Too Much of a Bad Thing

While cortisol is crucial for our survival, problems arise when its levels become imbalanced. Prolonged exposure to stress or chronic stress can lead to excessive cortisol production, resulting in a wide range of adverse effects on our physical and mental well-being.

1. **Fat Distribution:** Cortisol has been linked to weight gain, particularly in the abdominal area. High cortisol levels can increase appetite and lead to cravings for sugary, high-calorie foods. Moreover, cortisol stimulates the production of insulin, which promotes fat storage—especially visceral fat around the belly. This phenomenon explains why stress-related weight gain often manifests as excess belly fat.

2. **Immune System Suppression:** Elevated cortisol levels can weaken the immune system, making us more susceptible to infections and illnesses. Prolonged exposure to cortisol suppresses immune cells, reducing their ability to fight off pathogens effectively. Consequently, individuals with chronic stress may experience more frequent illnesses and slower recovery times.

3. **Brain Damage and Cognitive Function:** Excessive cortisol levels can have detrimental effects on brain health. Chronic stress and elevated cortisol have been associated with hippocampal atrophy, a condition characterized by the shrinking of the hippocampus—a region crucial for memory and learning. This can impair cognitive function, including memory recall, decision-making, and problem-solving abilities.

4. **Impact on Motivation:** Cortisol can also influence our motivation levels. While short bursts of cortisol can enhance focus and productivity, chronic elevation of cortisol can lead to a state of constant vigilance and hyper-vigilance. This heightened state of alertness can be draining, causing decreased motivation and a sense of fatigue or burnout.

Cortisol's Longevity in the System

Unlike the so-called "happy chemicals" in our bodies, which are swiftly metabolized and eliminated, *cortisol lingers in our system for a more extended period*. The body takes its time to break down cortisol, leading to a build-up over time when stress is persistent. This prolonged presence of cortisol can exacerbate its negative effects on various aspects of our physical and mental well-being.

Mother Natures Cortisol Support

Siberian Ginseng (Eleuthero)

Eleuthero has been researched for its potential to modulate the body's stress response (Panossian A, et al. "Adaptogens: a review of their history, biological activity, and clinical benefits." HerbalGram. 2013;96:52-63).

Holy Basil (Tulsi)

Studies have suggested that Tulsi may help in balancing cortisol levels and regulating the body's response to stress (Cohen MM. "Tulsi - Ocimum sanctum: A herb for all reasons." Journal of Ayurveda and integrative medicine. 2014;5(4):251).

Ashwaganda

In chronically stressed individuals, Ashwagandha has been shown to significantly reduce cortisol levels (Chandrasekhar K, et al. "A Prospective, Randomized Double-Blind, Placebo-Controlled Study of Safety and Efficacy of a High-Concentration Full-Spectrum Extract of Ashwagandha Root in Reducing Stress and Anxiety in Adults." Indian J Psychol Med. 2012;34(3):255-62).

Rhodiola Rosea

Rhodiola has been indicated in studies to help reduce cortisol and alleviate symptoms of fatigue and burnout (Olsson EM, et al. "A randomised, double-blind, placebo-controlled, parallel-group study of the standardised extract SHR-5 of the roots of Rhodiola rosea in the treatment of subjects with stress-related fatigue." Planta Med. 2009;75(2):105-12).

An adaptogen is a natural substance that helps the body adapt to stress and restores physiological balance.

It's important to consult with a healthcare professional before starting any new herbal supplement

FIVE ESSENTIAL ENHANCEMENTS

In today's fast-paced world, maintaining a healthy lifestyle can be challenging. With our busy schedules, it's easy to neglect the important aspects of our physical and mental health. However, by being aware of five essential enhancements, we can thrive and achieve a balanced and fulfilling lifestyle.

These enhancements include attitude, hydration, nutrition, playful activity, and body treatments such as massage, reiki, acupressure, and reflexology. By consciously incorporating these enhancements into our daily routine, we can shift our way of thinking and prioritize our well-being.

In this section, we will delve deeper into each of these enhancements and explore how they can contribute to a healthier lifestyle.

1. ATTITUDE

2. HYDRATION

3. NUTRITION

4. PLAYFUL ACTIVITY

5. BODY TREATMENTS

ATTITUDE

Attitude is one of the most important aspects that can affect our overall life satisfaction and daily energy levels. It is often said that our attitude determines our altitude. In aviation, attitude refers to the direction the wing of an aircraft leans to, which in turn determines the altitude the plane can reach. Similarly, our attitude in life can determine how high we can soar and achieve our goals.

Our attitude has a powerful impact on how we approach life and the energy we have throughout the day. It can either fuel us with enthusiasm and optimism or drain us of our energy and motivation. Our attitude also shapes our subconscious programming, which influences our thoughts, emotions, and behavior.

A negative attitude can focus our attention on the problems, obstacles, and failures in our lives, leading to feelings of stress, anxiety, and depression. On the other hand, a positive attitude can help us focus on the possibilities, opportunities, and successes, leading to feelings of happiness, joy, and contentment.

An attitude of gratitude is especially crucial to our overall life satisfaction and daily energy levels. When we cultivate gratitude and focus on the things we are thankful for, we attract positive energy into our lives. Gratitude helps us appreciate what we have, instead of focusing on what we lack. This leads to a more positive outlook on life, greater resilience, and increased overall well-being.

Our attitude is a critical factor in determining our life experience. By cultivating a positive attitude and an attitude of gratitude, we can shift our subconscious programming and attract positive energy into our lives. This, in turn, can lead to increased daily energy levels and greater overall life satisfaction.

HYDRATION

Hydration is a crucial factor in maintaining high energy levels throughout the day and overall life satisfaction. Water is essential for the proper functioning of our bodies, and a lack of hydration can cause a range of negative effects such as fatigue, headaches, and decreased mental performance. However, when it comes to hydration, it's not just about the quantity of water we drink, but also the quality.

There are three basic forms of water: purified, spring, and distilled. When it comes to purified water, we need to question whether it has the vital trace minerals found in nature. **Purified water** is processed to remove contaminants and impurities, but often the natural minerals are removed as well. It's important to ensure that the purified water we consume has added minerals to replenish those that were lost during the purification process.

In regards to **spring water**, we need to evaluate where the spring is located and look at the quality of the water itself. The quality of water from a spring can vary greatly depending on its location and the surrounding environment. For example, water from the island of Fiji, where the water has a long way to travel through the mountains to become purified, is a lot different than the near swamp waters of Zephyrhills Florida water.

Distilled water is another form of water that should be consumed with caution. Distilled water is stripped of all its minerals and, like the Chinese adage, "the pond that is too pure can hold no fish," distilled water is not recommended for regular consumption.

Our tap water may be purified with reverse osmosis, but this water may not only contain near-toxic levels of chlorine, it will also have other things like fluoride in it.

THE QUALITY OF WATER SHOULD BE PURE AND SHOULD INCLUDE THE NATURAL MINERALS LIKE CALCIUM, MAGNESIUM, AND ZINC TO BE CONSIDERED HEALTHY WATER, NOT JUST SAFE.

In addition to the quality of water, the quantity of water should also be regarded. This is different for each individual based upon various factors, such as weight, physical activity, and where they live. Drinking enough water is essential for maintaining optimal hydration levels, but over-hydration can also be harmful. It's essential to find a balance that works for your body and lifestyle.

Maintaining proper hydration is essential for high energy levels and overall life satisfaction. However, it's not just about drinking enough water but also ensuring the water we consume is of high quality, with the necessary minerals to support our bodies' functions. It's crucial to find the right balance of both quality and quantity to ensure optimal hydration and health.

NUTRITION

Proper nutrient-dense meals are the foundation of a healthy and energized life. However, with so many diets and food trends, it can be overwhelming to know where to start.

Keeping things simple is key to consistent success. The first step is to recondition ourselves away from fast food and the idea that it is the most convenient and least expensive option. In reality, preparing our meals with wholesome ingredients can be both affordable and convenient with a little planning and preparation.

Dr. Andreas Eenfeldt, a prominent advocate for low-carb and ketogenic diets, has significantly contributed to our understanding of satiety and the hedonic factor of foods. At the crux of his work is the idea that by choosing foods with high satiety and a low hedonic factor, individuals can naturally feel full and satisfied, eliminating the constant struggle with hunger and cravings.

This shifts the focus from relying heavily on willpower, which can often lead to feelings of deprivation and eventually to overeating. Instead, by making strategic food choices, one can essentially *'hack' their hunger*, leading to sustainable and healthy eating habits.

Low Satiety and High Hedonic Factor:

▶ Donuts
▶ Chips and crisps
▶ Candy bars
▶ Sugary sodas
▶ Ice cream

High Satiety and Low Hedonic Factor:

▶ Eggs
▶ Lean meats like chicken or turkey
▶ Green leafy vegetables
▶ Whole grains like quinoa or barley
▶ Avocado

By opting for the latter group of foods, the body receives ample nutrients and sustained energy, curbing the impulse to reach for empty-calorie, hyper-palatable foods that often lead to overconsumption and weight gain.

There are many different ways to discover what kind of eating patterns and foods will be most congruent with a healthy, energized life. For example, *Ayurveda and Chinese medicine* are ancient systems that are based on qualities and quantities, taking into account the individual and environmental climate. It's important to note that many modern diets can be too restrictive to be long-term successful. It's important to find a way of eating that is both sustainable and enjoyable, with a variety of nutrient-dense foods.

When you make decisions for what you eat, don't just think in terms of calories or fat or protein. Other factors greatly determine the end result of what happens when we eat something. Thinking in terms of foods, satiety - how full does it make you? Proteins makes you feel full quicker than carbs. Hedonic factor - how pleasurable is it to eat? Foods that have a lot of salt, fat and sugar are very hedonic ***and you can stop eating.***

Overall, the key to maintaining a healthy and energized lifestyle through proper nutrition is to keep it simple, enjoyable, and sustainable. It's important to find a way of eating that nourishes the body and mind, with a variety of nutrient-dense foods and a focus on enjoyment of the smell and taste of food.

With a little planning and preparation, anyone can create a healthy and energized way of eating that supports overall life satisfaction and daily energy levels.

PLAYFUL ACTIVITY

Our movement and activity levels have a significant impact on our energy levels and overall life satisfaction. Physical activity is essential for maintaining a healthy body and mind. However, it's important to note that not all types of movement are created equal. The type of activity we engage in matters just as much as the quantity.

Physical activity needs to be enjoyable and playful to truly reap its benefits. If we force ourselves to do an activity we don't enjoy, our bodies may not receive the full benefit we are looking for. This is because when we engage in activities we enjoy, we release endorphins, which are chemicals that promote feelings of pleasure and happiness. Endorphins help to reduce stress and improve our mood, which ultimately leads to increased energy levels and overall life satisfaction.

On the other hand, when we feel pressured or stressed during physical activity, we release cortisol, a hormone that promotes stress and anxiety. High levels of cortisol can lead to increased belly fat, which is not only unhealthy but also negatively impacts our self-esteem. Therefore, it's important to choose activities that bring us joy and avoid those that cause undue stress or pressure.

Regardless of the type of activity we engage in, we need to approach it with a playful and considerate mindset, like we did during playtime as children. This means we should have fun and not take ourselves too seriously. Playful activity can include anything from dancing, hiking, playing sports, or simply going for a walk. The key is to find what we enjoy and to make it a regular part of our lives.

Physical activity is essential for maintaining optimal energy levels and overall life satisfaction. However, not all movement is created equal. We need to engage in activities we enjoy and approach them with a playful and considerate mindset. This will help to promote the release of endorphins, reduce stress, and ultimately lead to a healthier and happier life.

BODY TREATMENTS

Body treatments are an important aspect of maintaining our bodies' happiness and overall life satisfaction. Massages and other body treatments have been proven to help keep the body balanced, moving freely, and pain-free. Not only do these treatments have positive effects on our physical health, but they also have positive effects on our mental and emotional states.

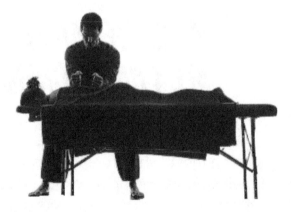

Massage therapy, for example, has been shown to reduce stress, anxiety, and depression. It also helps to improve circulation, reduce inflammation, and promote relaxation. Regular massage therapy can also keep a person out of expensive medical bills by helping to prevent chronic pain and other conditions.

Massage therapy can also help us increase energy levels through metabolic exchange. During a massage, circulation is improved, which helps to deliver oxygen and nutrients to the cells more efficiently. This, in turn, helps to increase our energy levels and promote overall health.

In addition, massages help to release the "four happy chemicals": endorphins, serotonin, dopamine, and oxytocin. In the section on motivation earlier in this chapter, we examined how these chemicals influence our motivation and good feeling in life.

MASSAGE CAN SAFELY RELEASE ALL 4 HAPPY CHEMICALS

There are many different types of body treatments available, and even those who are uncomfortable with the idea of taking off their clothes and being exposed can still find some type of treatment that will help their body repair and relax. For example, reflexology and acupressure can be done while fully clothed, and these treatments can also help to reduce stress and promote relaxation.

CONGRATULATIONS!

Throughout this book, we embarked on a transformative hero's journey of self-discovery.

In **Chapter One**, we explored the concept of lifestyle architecture, understanding that our lives are like intricate structures that can be intentionally designed. We discovered that we have the power to shape our lives and create a blueprint that aligns with our deepest values and priorities.

In **Chapter Two**, we studied the process of creating a lifestyle blueprint. By introspecting and reflecting on our desires, passions, and aspirations, we were able to construct a vision for our ideal life. We recognized the importance of authenticity, ensuring that our blueprint reflected our true selves, rather than conforming to societal expectations or external pressures.

Chapter Three shed light on the significance of our beliefs in shaping our lifestyle architecture. We realized that each belief we hold acts as a brick, contributing to the foundation of our chosen lifestyle. By questioning and challenging our limiting beliefs, we gained the freedom to construct a more empowering and expansive framework for our lives.

The journey continued in **Chapter Four**, where we explored the four pillars of lifestyle congruence: Chorus, cash, company and condition. We understood that true fulfillment comes from aligning these pillars with our values and ensuring harmony among them.

By appraising our lives and making necessary adjustments, we aimed for a life that is balanced, purpose-driven, and congruent with our deepest aspirations.

Finally, in **Chapter Five**, we examined the essential aspects of maintenance. We learned that sustaining our chosen lifestyle requires ongoing effort and commitment. Just like any architectural masterpiece, our lives require regular attention, care, and fine-tuning. We discovered the importance of self-care, setting boundaries, nurturing healthy habits, and cultivating a supportive environment that fosters growth and fulfillment.

As we conclude this book, let us remember that lifestyle architecture is a continuous journey. Our lives are dynamic, and as we grow and evolve, our blueprint may require revisions and adaptations. It is vital to remain open to change, embrace new experiences, and be willing to reassess our values and priorities along the way.

By integrating the principles of lifestyle architecture into our lives, we empower ourselves to design a life of purpose, freedom, and sustainable happiness. We have the ability to create a life that aligns with our deepest desires and values, one that brings us joy, fulfillment, and a sense of meaning.

May this book serve as a guide and source of inspiration as you embark on your own journey of lifestyle architecture. Remember, you hold the blueprint, and with each intentional decision, you are crafting a life that is uniquely yours. Embrace the power within you, and may your life become a testament to the transformative potential of intentional living.

DESIGN YOUR LIFE, BUILD YOUR DREAMS, AND REVEAL THE INCREDIBLE PERSON YOU WERE MEANT TO BE.

ABOUT THE AUTHOR
JOSHUAH "SHU" SHUMELDA

Shu is a seasoned speaker, teacher, and licensed massage therapist renowned for simplifying complex subjects. With over two decades in education, he's taught various subjects from anatomy to psychology across all grade levels.

A second-generation practitioner, Shu combines inherited wisdom with his training, offering profound insights into the human psyche and body.

He is well-versed in archetypal psychology, cognitive behavioral therapy, and is certified in neurolinguistic programming. This unique skill set enables him to guide individuals through transformative personal development, helping them address the "issues in the tissues," the "pain in the brain," and the "hurt in the heart."

Shu's dynamic speaking engagements range from colleges to the governor's safety and health conferences. His book, "How to Design a Life of Purpose, Freedom, and Sustainable Happiness," encapsulates his teachings on personal growth. His clear explanations, and compassionate nature make him a go-to expert for those seeking purposeful and happy lives.

In the heart of the earth, pressure births not only the luminous diamond but also the stoic granite and the elegant marble. It isn't mere pressure that crafts the brilliance of a diamond, but its unique dance of molecules.

Similarly, in the crucible of life's trials, it's not just the weight of our struggles that defines us, but the essence of our spirit and the facets of our character.

To evolve from mere stone to a radiant gem, we must possess not only resilience but also a profound understanding of our true nature, refining and polishing ourselves with intention.

In this journey to sculpt a life of purpose, freedom, and sustainable happiness, may we all find our inner diamond.

-Shu

Made in the USA
Las Vegas, NV
30 August 2023

76844084R00085